YEAR **B**
ADVENT/CHRISTMAS/EPIPHANY

YEAR **B**

ADVENT/CHRISTMAS/EPIPHANY

PREACHING

THE REVISED

COMMON

LECTIONARY

MARION SOARDS
THOMAS DOZEMAN
KENDALL McCABE

ABINGDON PRESS
Nashville

Preaching the Revised Common Lectionary
Year B: Advent/Christmas/Epiphany

Copyright © 1993 by Abingdon Press

This book is printed on recycled, acid-free paper.

Library of Congress Cataloging-in-Publication Data

Soards, Marion L., 1952-
    Preaching the revised common lectionary : year B / Marion Soards, Thomas
Dozeman, Kendall McCabe.
    p.   cm.
    Contents: [1] Advent/Christmas/Epiphany.
    ISBN 0-687-33802-6 (alk. paper)
    1. Bible—Homiletical use. 2. Lectionary preaching. 3. Advent. 4. Christmas.
5. Epiphany season. I. Dozeman, Thomas B. II. McCabe, Kendall, 1939-   .
III. Common lectionary (1992) IV. Title.
BS 534.5.S63   1993
251—dc20   92-36840
                                                                       CIP

Scripture quotations, unless otherwise noted, are from the New Revised Standard Version
of the Bible, copyright © 1989 by the Division of Christian Education of the National
Council of the Churches of Christ in the USA. Used by permission.

MANUFACTURED IN THE UNITED STATES OF AMERICA

Contents

CONTENTS

This is one volume in a twelve-volume series. Each volume contains commentary and worship suggestions for a portion of lectionary cycle A, B, or C. Since the lections for a few special days do not change from one lectionary cycle to another, material for each of these days appears in only one of the volumes. Appropriate cross references in the table of contents lead the reader to material in other volumes of the series.

Introduction

Now pastors and students have a systematic treatment of essential issues of the Christian year and Bible study for worship and proclamation based on the Revised Common Lectionary. Interpretation of the lectionary will separate into three parts: Calendar, Canon, and Celebration. A brief word of introduction will provide helpful guidelines for utilizing this resource in worship through the Christian year.

Calendar. Every season of the Christian year will be introduced with a theological interpretation of its meaning, and how it relates to the overall Christian year. This section will also include specific liturgical suggestions for the season.

Canon. The lectionary passages will be interpreted in terms of their setting, structure, and significance. First, the word *setting* is being used loosely in this commentary to include a range of different contexts in which biblical texts can be interpreted from literary setting to historical or cultic settings. Second, regardless of how the text is approached under the heading of setting, interpretation will always proceed to an analysis of the structure of the text under study. Third, under the heading of significance, central themes and motifs of the passage will be underscored to provide a theological interpretation of the text as a springboard for preaching. Thus interpretation of the lectionary passages will result in the outline on the next page.

Celebration. This section will focus on specific ways of relating the lessons to liturgical acts and/or homiletical options for the day on which they occur. How the texts have been used in the Christian tradition will sometimes be illustrated to stimulate the thinking of preachers and planners of worship services.

I. OLD TESTAMENT TEXTS

A. The Old Testament Lesson

1. Setting

2. Structure

3. Significance

B. Psalm

1. Setting

2. Structure

3. Significance

II. NEW TESTAMENT TEXTS

A. The Epistle

1. Setting

2. Structure

3. Significance

B. The Gospel

1. Setting

2. Structure

3. Significance

Why We Use the Lectionary

Although many denominations have been officially or unofficially using some form of the lectionary for many years, some pastors are still unclear about where it comes from, why some lectionaries differ from denomination to denomination, and why the use of a lectionary is to be preferred to a more random sampling of scripture.

Simply put, the use of a lectionary provides a more diverse scriptural diet for God's people, and it can help protect the congregation from the whims and prejudices of the pastor and other worship planners. Faithful use of the lectionary means that preachers must deal with texts they had rather ignore, but about which the congregation may have great concern and interest. An apocalyptic text, such as we encounter in this volume on the First Sunday of Advent, might be a case in point. Adherence to the lectionary can be an antidote to that homiletical arrogance that says, "I know what my people need," and in humility acknowledges that the Word of God found in scripture may speak to more needs on Sunday morning than we even know exist, when we seek to proclaim faithfully the message we have wrestled from the text.

The lectionary may also serve as a resource for liturgical content. The psalm is intended to be a response to the Old Testament lesson, and not read as a lesson itself, but beyond that the lessons may inform the content of prayers of confession, intercession, and petition. Some lessons may be adapted as affirmations of faith, as in *The United Methodist Hymnal,* nos. 887-889; the United Church of Christ's *Hymnal* nos. 429-30; and the Presbyterian *Worshipbook,* no. 30. The "Celebration" entries for each day will call attention to these opportunities from time to time.

Pastors and preachers in the free-church tradition should think of the lectionary as a primary resource for preaching and worship, but need to remember that the lectionary was made for them and not they for the lectionary. The lectionary may serve as the inspiration for a separate series of lessons and sermons that will include texts not in the present

9

edition, or having chosen one of the lectionary passages as the basis for the day's sermon, the preacher may wish to make an independent choice of the other lessons to supplement and illustrate the primary text. The lectionary will be of most value when its use is not a cause for legalism but for inspiration. Pastors who experience a love/hate relationship with the lectionary will gain much sympathy and guidance from Eugene L. Lowry's penetrating analysis in *Living With the Lectionary: Preaching Through the Revised Common Lectionary* (Nashville: Abingdon Press, 1992).

Just as there are no perfect preachers, there are no perfect lectionaries. The Revised Common Lectionary, upon which this series is based, is the result of the work of many years by the Consultation on Common Texts and is a response to on-going evaluation of the Common Lectionary (1983) by pastors and scholars from the several participating denominations. The current interest in the lectionary can be traced back to the Second Vatican Council, which ordered lectionary revision for the Roman Catholic Church:

> The treasures of the Bible are to be opened up more lavishly, so that richer fare may be provided for the faithful at the table of God's Word. In this way a more representative portion of the holy Scriptures will be read to the people over a set cycle of years. (Walter Abbott, ed., *The Documents of Vatican II*, [Piscataway, N.J.: New Century, 1974] p. 155)

The example thus set by Roman Catholics inspired Protestants to take more seriously the place of the Bible in their services and sermons, and soon many denominations had issued their own three-year cycles, based generally on the Roman Catholic model but with their own modifications. This explains why some discrepancies and variations appear in different forms of the lectionary. The Revised Common Lectionary (RCL) is an effort to increase agreement among the churches. A table at the end of the volume will list the differences between the RCL and the Roman Catholic, Episcopal, and Lutheran lectionaries. Where no entry is made, all are in agreement with the RCL .

For those unacquainted with the general pattern of the lectionary, a brief word of explanation may be helpful for sermon preparation. (1) The three years are each distinguished by one of the Synoptic Gospels: Matthew in A, Mark in B, Luke in C. John is distributed over the three years with a heavy emphasis during Lent and Easter. (2) Two types of readings are used. During the periods of Advent to Epiphany and Lent to Pentecost, the readings are usually topical, that is, there is some common theme among them. During the Sundays after Epiphany and Pentecost the readings are continuous, with no necessary connection between the lessons. In the period covered by this volume (Advent, Christmas, Epiphany), there is a thematic connection between the Old Testament lesson and the Gospel during the Sundays After Epiphany, but the epistle lesson begins a series of readings from I and II Corinthians. The preacher begins, then, with at least four preaching options: to deal with either one of the lessons on their own or to work with the dialogue between the Old Testament lesson and the Gospel. Perhaps it should also be added that though the psalm is intended to be a response by the people to the Old Testament lesson—rather than as a lesson on its own—this in no way suggests that it cannot be used as the text for the sermon.

This is the first of four volumes that deal with the lessons for the entire B Cycle of the Christian year. The second volume will include Ash Wednesday through the Day of Pentecost. The third volume begins with Trinity Sunday (the First Sunday After Pentecost) and includes all the lessons for June, July, and August. The fourth volume finishes the remainder of the year, including the lessons for Thanksgiving Day. A new series will then be published for the C Cycle. Four volumes have already been published for Year A. They contain commentaries on the First Proper of Christmas (vol. 1), and the Easter Vigil (vol. 2) which, because they are the same for all three years, are not duplicated in this series.

A note on language: We have used the term *Old Testament* in this series because that is the language employed by the Consultation on Common Texts, at least up to this point. Pastors and worship committees may wish to consider alternative terms such as *First Testament* or *Hebrew Scriptures* that do not imply that those writings somehow have less value than the rest of the Christian Bible. Another option is to refer to *First Lesson* (always from the Hebrew Scriptures), *Second Lesson* (from Acts, Revelation, or the epistles), and *Gospel*.

THE PASCHAL MYSTERY AND ADVENT

Preachers and liturgical planners who seek to take seriously the Christian year as the basis of their work need to remember first of all that the purpose for the year is to allow us to focus on particular aspects of the Easter proclamation and their relevance to Christian life and thought. Easter is at the center of the Christian faith; without Easter there could be no Christian faith, only the Good Friday memory of a man who tried valiantly to make a witness about God and failed. The Christian year grew out of the Church's desire to participate as fully as possible in every aspect of the Paschal mystery by dynamically remembering and thus sharing in the salvation-giving events recorded in scripture.

Thus understood, the observance of the Christian year is not the same as the annual cyclical celebrations of the Greco-Roman mystery religions. In the mystery religions, the gods needed to have the ritual activities performed in order to assist them in bringing about the salvation of the performers; the gods were dependent upon the worshipers for their very existence. It was the activity of the faithful that brought the god back to life. In Christian worship, we acknowledge what God has done and is doing by virtue of God's own will and power. So for Christians, the Resurrection is a fact proclaimed and experienced, rather than a need of God that the worshiper is called upon to help bring about. God is responsible for the Easter triumph, not us or even our faith in the Resurrection.

This means that the Church does not approach Advent pretending that Jesus has not yet been born or that we know nothing about Calvary and the empty tomb. Advent is celebrated in the light of the Christ-event; it is an examination and celebration of the Easter mystery from this side of the empty tomb. We do not sing Christmas carols or preach sermon series on "They Met at the Manger" during Advent because we are ignorant of Christmas, but because we wish to experience and proclaim that hope which in Israel waited in faith for the Messiah during the darkest and most desolate of times, and which since Easter still waits in "for the revealing of our Lord Jesus Christ" (I Corinthians 1:7, Second Reading, First Sunday of Advent, Year B).

Advent is the Janus of the Christian year. It looks backward at Israel's expectation of a Messiah (the Old Testament lessons), and it looks forward to the consummation, to the ultimate triumph of Christ over the power of sin and death that was begun on that first Easter Day. Advent, in its message of judgment and the reign of Christ, is as much a result of Easter as it is an anticipation of Easter and may be considered the end of the Christian year as appropriately as it is considered the beginning. Because we mortals are linear beings, creatures of time, we usually want things to have a beginning and an end. Because Advent does deal with the expectation of the Messiah and the preparations for his birth, there is a logic in using it to begin the annual cycle.

Once again, we must remember that this is not a cyclic event as in the mystery religions, where the god is dependent upon our actions for his or her existence, and where the same event occurs over and over again. We may use the term *cycle* as a matter of convenience, but the fact is that we are not the same persons who celebrated Advent last year, and we are not the same persons who will celebrate Advent next year. Yearly we bring another 365 days of grace to our celebration, and so our insight into the Paschal mystery is deeper and our observance conditioned by the previous year's "dangers, toils, and fears." We are not the same people doing the same thing year after year. The hope we bring to this year's Advent is not the same hope we brought last year, for it has been tempered and informed by "the encouragement of the scriptures" (Romans 15:4, Second Reading, Second Sunday of Advent, Year A), as during the year we have sought to "put on the Lord Jesus Christ" (Romans 13:14, Second Reading, First Sunday of Advent, Year A).

The Liturgical Environment

Colors. Purple has been the customary color for Advent in the Western Church since the sixteenth century. There has been a recent trend to the use of blue, based on the inventories of some medieval churches. Rigidity over the use of color did not come about until the Reformation, when the invention of printing allowed worship to be rubricized and regulated. The catalogs of publishing houses notwithstanding, purple is not primarily a color of penitence; that is a symbolism attached to the color after the fact, once purple had been assigned to Lent and then to Advent. The penitential character of Lent gave symbolic interpretation to the color. In the ancient world, purple was the color of royalty, since only a royal income could afford the dye that made it possible. Purple, then, points to the kingship of Christ, "the Lord's anointed, great David's greater Son." We decorate our churches in purple or royal blue (not a pastel blue) to prepare for the coming of the king.

The use of a pink candle in the Advent wreath is an imitation of a Roman Catholic practice that is not even required of churches outside the city of Rome itself. The observance of Lent/Easter is older than that of Advent/Christmas, and so the liturgical practices of the latter tended to be modeled on those that had developed earlier for the former. An idiosyncracy in the Roman practice developed because by the early Middle Ages the custom had developed for the pope, as a sign of special favor, to give a golden rose to persons he especially esteemed. He did this on the Fourth Sunday in Lent, and in honor of the occasion the churches were decorated with rose-colored paraments. The day came to be seen as a respite before plunging into the rigors of the last days of the Lenten fast. It also helped that the first word of the introit for that Sunday was "laetare," rejoice. Because Advent was looked upon as a "little Lent," it became the custom on the third Sunday (when the first word of the introit was "gaudete," also rejoice!) to use rose vestments to parallel the Lenten pattern.

Advent wreaths. Advent wreaths have become popular visual aids in many churches to mark the time through Advent, and the making of them provides activities for the church school, family nights, and similar meetings. Often the products are then used as a part of individual or family devotions throughout the season. Family units are often employed to do the lighting of the wreath at the beginning of the church service each Sunday. (Pastors might want to examine what kind of silent judgment this pronounces against single persons. Is it a reinforcement of the popular myth that "Christmas is only for children" or that the season can only be appreciated in a family context?)

Please note that the various candles on the Advent wreath don't mean anything! As Archibald MacLeish said about poetry, "An Advent wreath should not mean, but be." Symbolization, the attribution of one meaning to a thing which does not in itself evoke that meaning, is a frequent liturgical error; we inhibit or restrict meaning by insisting that things should mean only the one thing we arbitrarily assign to them. If individuals or groups are going to prepare their own liturgies for the lighting of the wreath, and insist on attributing meaning to each candle, then the meaning (or more accurately, the theme) should grow out of a consideration of the lessons for the day, and that theme may appropriately change from year to year.

Chrismons. A more recent appearance has been made in many churches by chrismon trees hung with symbols of Christ. It is difficult to avoid the suspicion that these are a means of sneaking Christmas trees onto the scene early. If they are to be used at all, they certainly should not be evergreens. It would be preferable to use something of bare branches only. Following the same logic, the hanging of the greens is inappropriate before the Fourth Sunday of Advent, no matter how close to Christmas itself that may be. The absence of any altar flowers during these four Sundays can be a remarkable contrast to the explosion of poinsettias that is to come.

Silence. Advent is a time to encourage the use of silence. Waiting and watching are major themes of the season, and they can be reinforced by ritual silence that should stand in marked contrast to the musical merriment of the Christmas celebration. Roman Catholic, Lutheran, and Anglican churches have customarily suppressed the use of the *Gloria in excelsis Deo* ("Glory be to God on high") during Advent, so that this song of the angels is heard with a fresh appreciation at the first service of Christmas. An absence of organ voluntaries may also be appropriate.

A hymn. The hymn, "O Come, O Come, Emmanuel," and the "O" antiphons on which it is based, provide a number of significant images for use as Advent visuals on bulletins, paraments, vestments, and so on. (Different versions include no. 211 in *The United Methodist Hymnal;* no. 56 in the Episcopal *The Hymnal, 1982,* and pages 174-75 in *The Lutheran Book of Worship.*) Among them are a crown and scepter for the expected king, a key, a star of David, a Jesse tree, and a rising sun. The application of the title "Wisdom" (Sophia or Sapientia) to Christ in the text of "O Come, O Come, Emmanuel" reminds us of the sexual inclusiveness of redemption since Wisdom has often been portrayed as a female. This use is also found in the hymn "O Word of God Incarnate."

Because "O Come, O Come, Emmanuel" is so rich with images, its use ought not be restricted to once during the season (particularly now that many hymnals include seven rather than four stanzas!). The stanzas might be divided among the Sundays and used as a part of the lighting of the Advent wreath or some other act of worship. This would allow a familiar Advent hymn to be used each Sunday and would permit more time to explore one or two Advent images more fully. The stanzas of the hymn could be sung in response to the recitation of the complementary "O" antiphons. Stanza 1 alone would be used on the First Sunday of Advent, 2 and 3 on the Second Sunday, 4 and 5 on the Third Sunday, and 6 and 7 on the Fourth Sunday. An appropriate collect could conclude the rite, particularly if the lighting of the wreath is also the opening act of worship.

First Sunday of Advent

Old Testament Texts

The Old Testament lessons explore the dark side of Advent. Isaiah 64:1-9 and Psalm 80:1-7, 17-19 are communal laments that raise the question of whether the waiting for God will ever end.

The Lesson: *Isaiah 64:1-9*

"Waiting for Godot"

Setting. Even though Isaiah 64:1-4 is placed within a prophetic book, it is less a prophetic oracle than a psalm. The text is part of a larger community lament that includes Isaiah 63:7–64:12. There is an aura of disillusionment and abandonment that permeates this writing, for the situation of the community is one in which God has not been present for some time and, indeed, is still absent during the use of the hymn. Scholars conclude from this that the hymn may have been a liturgical composition used for worship in the exilic period. Such a situation is certainly reflected by a series of questions that are addressed to God throughout the lamentation: Where are you? (63:11); Where is your salvation? (63:15); Why do you harden our hearts against you? (63:17); Will you continue to keep silent? (64:12). These questions explore the dark side of Advent, for the communal lament explores waiting—not simply as a process by which we reach a conclusion, but as an end unto itself.

Structure. If the lectionary reading is actually part of a larger psalm of lament, then Isaiah 63:7–64:12 can be outlined in the following manner, with a suggestive sermon apparent in the structure (look, return, come).

    I. Prophetic Recounting of God's Past Salvation (63:7-14)
   II. Communal Lamentation (63:15–64:12)
      A. Look down God! (63:15-16)

B. Return God! (63:17-19)

C. Come down God! (64:1-12)

The larger community lament begins with a recounting of God's past salvation from Egypt. The prophet underscores the central point that God suffered with Israel in Egypt even when they did know it (63:9). This fact, however, creates more problems than solutions, since it raises the first central question for the community of faith in the here and now, Where is this God of the Exodus? (v. 11). The absence of the God of the Exodus provides the context for the three pleas from the worshiping community, each of which is tied up with a question. The request for God to look down is linked with the question about God's power to save (v. 15). The request for God to return to Israel is interwoven with the question of why God let Israel stray in the first place (v. 17). Finally, the lectionary text takes the argument to its ultimate conclusion, for here God is requested to reappear and thus recreate the Exodus of old. But there is no divine appearance to these pleas for help and the psalm ends with a question rather than an answer, "Will you keep silent?" (64:12).

Significance. The structure of the communal lament in Isaiah 63:7–64:12 presents a challenge to the preacher. It is the First Sunday of Advent, and thus we begin the liturgical cycle anew. But it is not the first time that the worshipers have gone through this cycle and repetition of the liturgical year focuses the worshiping community too early on the outcome of our waiting in Advent to the celebration of Christmas. Yet Advent is not about Christmas, it is about waiting, which can be an end unto itself. And if we focus on Christmas too early, we turn Advent into something else altogether. The following illustration may provide insight into this point. Advent is not like waiting in a doctor's lobby for a flu shot when the doctor is running hours behind schedule. In such a situation waiting is a minor irritation, which is what Advent becomes when we focus on Christmas too early. Advent could also be conceived as a situation of waiting in a doctor's lobby with a potentially fatal case of pneumonia and not knowing for sure that there is even a doctor in the office. The communal lament in Isaiah 63:7–64:12 is more like the second example. It is riddled with real existential questions in which the worshiping community tries to locate God (63:11), then wonders if God is able to save (63:15), and finally questions whether the people are even salvageable (64:12).

The challenge to the preacher of Isaiah 63:7–64:12 is to convey this dark side of Advent (that waiting as an end in itself) is an acceptable mode of faith. In order to communicate the message of Isaiah 63:7–64:12, the preacher must make it clear that Advent is not about the discipline of having to wait in order to open presents on Christmas. Christmas does not appear in our Old Testament lesson.

Note how the text ends without an answer to the questions of faith. The ending of this text suggests that to question God in times of doubt through lamenting is in itself an act of faith that need not reach the goal of Christmas. Having said this, however, there is another danger in this text that must be avoided—namely, to idealize existential doubt or angst as the goal of the text. The larger boundaries of the lament provide an avenue for the preacher to avoid this danger and thus to rise above the level of Samuel Beckett's *Waiting for Godot.* Even though the God of the Exodus is presently absent, the past experience of the Exodus provides for a theological conclusion in 63:9 that goes beyond the present experience of the worshiping community. The conclusion is that God was present in the first Exodus to the point of sharing in the affliction of Israel in Egypt even when they did not know it. This past truth opens the possibility that the same thing might also be true for the present worshiping community. The shared suffering of God in our moments of lamenting—even when we are not aware are of it—allows for the possibility of having the waiting of Advent become an end unto itself.

The Response: *Psalm 80:1-7, 17-19*

A Prayer for Salvation

Setting. Psalm 80 maintains an analogous situation found in Isaiah 63:7–64:12. It, too, is a national lament in which the community of faith is pictured as waiting for the salvation of God and calling upon God to bring about a new salvation. Some scholars describe the genre of Psalm 80 as a song of communal prayer rather than a national lament, because of the use of the term *people's prayer* in v. 4. The implied situation of a communal prayer, however, is similar to that of a national lament in that it, too, presupposes a time of distress.

Structure. The lectionary reading is the first half of a larger psalm that can be outlined in four parts.

      I. A Plea for Help (vv. 1-3)

     II. A Description of Divine Anger (vv. 4-7)

III. A Recounting of Past Salvation (vv. 8-13)
IV. A Plea for Help (vv. 14-19)

Woven throughout the psalm are variations of the refrain, "Restore us, O God; let your face shine, that we may be saved" (vv. 3, 7, 19).

Significance. The refrains in vv. 3 and 7 provide the central theme for interpreting Psalm 80:1-7, 17-19. God is absent and the community undertakes a sustained effort to invoke God to return, so that they might be saved. The first part of the hymn explores imagery of God the shepherd to describe the character of salvation as that of being led by God. The second part of the hymn (vv. 4-7) describes the result of God's abandonment of the people. Weeping prevails within the community (v. 5) and oppression lurks outside (v. 6). This very direct and sustained plea for salvation in v. 1 provides a fitting counterpart and conclusion to the more introspective response to the problem of waiting that was presented in Isaiah 63:7–64:12.

New Testament Texts

The texts for this first Sunday in Advent bring together strikingly different passages from the early portions of Paul's letter to the Corinthians and from the final portions of Mark's account of Jesus' ministry (before the Passion account). The mention of the future "revelation of our Lord Jesus Christ" at "the end . . . in the day of our Lord" in I Corinthians and the clear future focus of the verses in Mark on the coming of the Son of Man and the unknown day and hour of his coming unite these Advent lessons.

The Epistle: *I Corinthians 1:3-9*

Living for Christ's Revelation

Setting. These verses of I Corinthians come from both the salutation (vv. 1-3) and the thanksgiving (vv. 4-9) of Paul's letter. Paul begins even in these initial portions of the letter to speak to the circumstances in Corinth. In general the situation is as follows: Some members of the church in Corinth are quarreling and forming competitive cliques, each of which claims to be more spiritual than the others. In short, spiritual arrogance is tearing apart the body of Christ as one group and then another demonstrates its spiritual superiority. Paul addresses this multifaceted mess, which has a unifying core—namely, the will to boast.

Structure. There are actually two distinct parts to this lesson. First, v. 3 comes from the salutation of the letter and is, in fact, the third element of the greeting: It is the salutation that follows the naming of the senders and the recipients of the letter. Second, vv. 4-9 offer an epistolary thanksgiving. The "grace and peace" from God and Christ in v. 3 actually create the theological context in which one is to read and interpret all that follows. Sermons that focus on the themes of vv. 4-9 (thanksgiving, divine enrichment, confirmation in the lives of believers of the testimony to Christ in Christian teaching and preaching, and divine sustaining in everyday life as believers live looking for the coming of the Lord) should establish a context or worldview of divine "grace and peace" in which to expound the themes of Paul's thanksgiving.

Significance. Something of the "real" meaning of grace and peace becomes clear from reading the opening of Paul's letter to the Corinthians in the light of information found in the Acts of the Apostles. In this letter Sosthenes is called Paul's brother, not because of any human bond, but because they have been united in Christ in a fraternal bond as children of God. This relationship is remarkable, for from Acts we learn that Sosthenes was the former leader of the Corinthian synagogue Jews who filed charges against Paul with the proconsul Gallio. Thus, in reality, human hostility and opposition were obliterated through radical divine reconciliation, so that grace and peace in human living flow from the mutual relationship of believers to God.

The greeting punctuating Paul's (and Sosthenes') salutation (v. 3) shows the degree to which Christian life and living have been radically reformed through the work of God in Christ. Paul (and Sosthenes) declare "grace and peace," not mere "greetings" to the Corinthian Christians. It is the difference between meeting the monarch of England and greeting her with "God save the Queen!" rather than "Hi." Grace is the work of God for the salvation of humankind, and peace is the result of God's labor in Jesus Christ.

In the thanksgiving (vv. 4-9) Paul signals the cause of both his joy and his concern for the Corinthians. God richly blessed these believers with "spiritual gifts," a topic of major concern in the body of this letter, but the Corinthians have misunderstood and abused God's blessings— as Christians too often do. Forgetting that God is the common source of whatever "spiritual gifts" they possess, the Corinthians behave as if they themselves were to be credited with their Christian capacities. Paul subtly reminds them that God granted them all that they have and are in

Christ and that they are called to steadfastness in Christ (not dissension) for God who is faithful sustains them (and us) as they (and we) live awaiting the day of our Lord Jesus Christ. Too often we "get ahead" of ourselves and forget that God's good gifts are given in order to sustain us in mutual love; they are not private matters that elevate us over one another.

As we live in the world, transformed in our relationships through our essential relationship to God, we live out a Christ-styled and Christ-oriented life. Our focus for living is not simply ourselves, but rather our Lord. His grace and peace give us the capacity to give up our natural tendency toward self-centeredness and instead to give ourselves in service to others, so that the testimony to Christ is confirmed among us (v. 6). This selfless quality of life is an active fellowship, not merely a wimpish doormat disposition, which is sustained by God's faithful work in, through, and among us!

The Gospel: *Mark 13:24-37*

Jesus and the Future of Believers

Setting. The reader of Mark's account of Jesus follows Jesus' ministry from its origins during the work of John the Baptist through its first phases in Galilee into Judea and, eventually, to Jerusalem. All along the way Jesus speaks and acts in an authoritative fashion, and he steadily debates with recognized religious authorities concerning the law and God's will. In Jerusalem the debates intensify, Jesus' activities become more controversial, and his teaching becomes enigmatically startling. Mark 13 forms a final section of teaching, particularly concerned with the future, that immediately precedes the large complex of thoroughly integrated stories that form the Passion narrative (Mark 14 and 15 [and 16?]).

Structure. Chapter 13 is a cluster of teachings about the future. Scholars do not think this section was delivered as a single continuous lesson; rather the materials in this chapter seem to come from different times and settings. But the common concern of these teachings with the future led to their collection on the principle that "like attracts like." Mark offers the section as a grand final pronouncement before the great climax of the Passion; yet, there are distinguishable units of material in the whole.

In the verses of this week's lesson, there are three clearly discernible parts: vv. 24-27—a section filled with apocalyptic images and concerned with the coming of the Son of Man; vv. 28-31—a set of sayings related to an imminent crisis; and vv. 32-37—teaching about the unknown time of final judgment and admonition to prudent, constant preparation. One, two, or all three of these sections could be the basis of a sermon on "divine judgment," "the promise of fulfillment," and/or "the call to readiness."

Significance. Part of the difficulty of interpreting Mark 13 is that the sections of this chapter deal with two distinct times of distress: the trauma of the destruction of Jerusalem and the crisis of final judgment at the end of time. Distinguishing these times from each other is a key to comprehending the message(s) in this lesson.

Verses 24-27 speak of final judgment. These verses are filled with vocabulary, images, and ideas from the Old Testament; and recognizing the allusions to such passages as Isaiah 13:10, 34:4; Joel 2:10, 3:4, 15; Daniel 7:13; Zechariah 2:6; and perhaps Deuteronomy 30:4 clarifies the meaning of the passage. The text speaks of God's ultimate, determinative judgment of humanity. The "Son of Man" recalls a significant figure from Daniel who judges in God's behalf; but, here, Mark reports Jesus' words in such a way that the Christian reader understands that the "Son of Man" is Jesus himself. The Son of Man who suffered, died, and was raised promises to come exercising divine judgment. Yet, the overall portrait of Jesus as the coming Son of Man depicts him in even greater glory than the figure in Daniel. The Christian expects Jesus to come, not merely in behalf of God, but indeed acting in the role of God. This is clear from the mention of his coming "in clouds with great power and glory," which is Old Testament language for God's own manner of appearing (see, e.g., Exodus 16:10; Psalm 104:1-3; Isaiah 19:1; and Ezekiel 30:1-3). Furthermore, it is the coming Son of Man who will send out the angels and gather the elect, two common Old Testament descriptions of the activity of God (see, e.g., Deuteronomy 30:1-4 and Zechariah 1:13-14). At the heart of these verses is the declaration that God will have final say over the destiny of creation. Christians understand that the crucified and resurrected Jesus will play the central role in God's promised judgment. Though tribulation is associated with Christ's coming, the prophecy of this passage should instill more hope than anxiety for believers.

Verses 28-31 refer to the forthcoming destruction of Jerusalem, as is clear from the phrases "these things taking place" and "this generation will not pass away before all these things take place." Signs foreshadowing the end ("these things," vv. 29-30) can hardly follow the end (vv. 24-27, 32-37). The seemingly strange sandwiching of references to Jerusalem's destruction between statements about final judgment is Mark's way of saying that the surety of the end is as certain as the fate of Jerusalem. In preaching, one can follow Mark's lead and speak of the promise of judgment in relation to real signs of God's judgment in the course of history; and, again, these are primarily words of assurance, not threat.

Finally, Jesus' words in vv. 32-37 about the time of the end may prove dissatisfying or frustrating to any who want to read scripture as a crystal ball. Yet, Jesus words are crystal clear! The time of the end is unknown to all except God, and this is even the case for Jesus himself. Nevertheless, that the time of the end is unknown and, therefore, unpredictable does not mean that the promise of final judgment is irrelevant. Indeed, because the time is unknown, believers are to be constantly prepared. Those who believe that Jesus is coming are to live in expectation that molds the form and gives quality to everyday living. Christian hope energizes faithful Christian living.

ADVENT 1: THE CELEBRATION

Waiting is the theme that appears throughout today's lessons, and it sets the tone for the Advent observance. Two kinds of waiting are involved during this season: first, there is the waiting for the parousia, Christ's triumphant appearance in glory, which is emphasized today, and second, there is the waiting for Christmas, which becomes an increasing focus until we hear the Annunciation story on the Fourth Sunday of Advent. Each aspect needs to be given proper attention if the liturgy is to help us identify ourselves as those who are living between the times (see Old Testament commentary above).

Today can be considered as much an end of the Christian year as its beginning (see comments about Advent's Janus-like character above). During the last Sundays in Year A the lessons dealt with the parables of judgment in Matthew 25, and today a climax is reached in the reading from Mark's apocalypse. We complete a thematic unit from one year as we begin another year. The preacher may wish to point this out to underscore how the observance of the Christian year is a pattern of growth and not mere repetition of the same old thing.

The waiting that is described in today's lessons is an active, not a passive thing. It is not a thumb-twiddling, "everything's-going-to-be-fine" attitude that absolves us of any need to participate in the world. As the commentator on the Gospel concludes, "Christian hope energizes faithful Christian living." What does it mean to be the slaves who are left in charge? It may be helpful to remember that this Sunday will generally fall close to December 1, the anniversary of the day in 1955 on which Rosa Parks refused to give up her bus seat to a person of another race, and thus inaugurated a contemporary example of active waiting. This commemoration may provide part of the prayer agenda for today's service if not a sermon illustration.

The corporate character of the lessons and the liturgy needs to be emphasized as an antidote to the tendency to think of judgment only as negative and only as individual. The Christian hope is that it is the Crucified One, the divine One who suffered from human judgment, who will settle accounts, and that is good news! The Church, the fellowship of the redeemed, waits for the judgment of Christ in hope and confidence, because the Church knows herself to be beloved by Christ. That is why "the Spirit and the bride say, 'Come'" (Revelation 22:17) in joyous expectation and not in fear. The Church can sing with Walt Whitman (but in another frame of reference):

> My foothold is tenon'd and mortis'd in granite,
> I laugh at what you call dissolution,
> And I know the amplitude of time.
> (*Song of Myself*, lines 419-421)

The Gospel reference to the elect (the Church) being gathered from the four winds is incorporated into one of the oldest extant liturgical compositions, the Didache (10:5-6). The following adaptation of it may serve as a prayer before the benediction during the whole season of Advent.

Remember, Lord, your Church,
to save it from all evil and to make it perfect by your love.
Make it holy,
and gather it together from the four winds
into your Kingdom which you have made ready for it.
Let Grace come and let this world pass away.
Hosanna to the God of David!
Our Lord, come!
Amen.
[Cyril Richardson, ed., *Early Christian Fathers* (Philadelphia: Westminster, 1953), p. 176]

27

The hymn "Have Thine Own Way, Lord" picks up the pot and potter image from Isaiah and so can serve as a response to that lesson. The Old Testament lesson may also be used to create a call to confession or a prayer of confession for this day, which may be repeated throughout the season.

If the Eucharist is celebrated on this day to mark the beginning of the Christian year, the preacher may wish to draw attention to Paul's opening words in the epistle about giving thanks (eucharisto) as a kind of active waiting, which characterizes the Christian life and helps establish Christian identity.

Second Sunday of Advent

Old Testament Texts

The Old Testament readings address one of the common problems of the Advent season, which was described last week—when waiting becomes an end in itself. In an attempt to address this problem, each text presents a message of salvation and hope to a people who have sunk into a state of hopelessness.

The Lesson: *Isaiah 40:1-11*

You Can't Always Trust What You Feel

Setting. The following commentary is also meant to be used for Isaiah 40:21-31 on the Fifth Sunday of Epiphany. Two important insights concerning the setting of Isaiah 40 will aid in interpreting the text. First, the literary setting or structure fits the genre of a prophetic call. This structure was introduced in the call of Moses in Exodus 3:1-15 (First Reading, Year A, Proper 17) and touched upon again in the call of Gideon in Judges 6:1-12 (13-17) (First Reading, Year A, Proper 27). The form of a prophetic call narrative often separates into six parts, which consist of (1) divine confrontation, (2) introductory word, (3) commission, (4) objection, (5) reassurance, and (6) sign. The insight concerning literary form raises two questions: Who is being called? And, what is the context of the call? The questions are puzzling because the prophet Isaiah, who lived in the seventh century B.C.E., was called or drafted into service in Isaiah 6 (a text which also fits the genre of a call narrative). Furthermore the social setting of the prophetic call in Isaiah 40 is not the over-confidence of seventh century Israel that prevails in Isaiah 6, but a feeling of despair about whether God is present and concerned at all for Israel. Scripture scholars, for this and other reasons, have concluded that Isaiah 40 is the call of an anonymous prophet ("Second Isaiah") during the time of the exile in the sixth century B.C.E.

Isaiah 40:27 describes the situation in terms of overwhelming doubt—bordering on nihilism—to which this new and different Isaiah is being called. His audience believes that "[their] way is hidden from the LORD, and [their] right is disregarded by [their] God." The loss of an entire nation through mass deportation provides strong experiential confirmation of the truth of Israel's nihilism. Thus the challenge for Second Isaiah is to present a message of hope in a situation that is clearly hopeless. In order to do this he must critically evaluate the religious experience of Israel in the exile. He must answer the question of whether God is, in fact, more than the sum total of their present experience.

Structure. Isaiah 40:1-11 plays with the genre of a prophetic call. It follows the form loosely:

      I.   Divine Confrontation (vv. 1-2)
     II.   Introductory Word (vv. 3-5)
    III.   Commission (v. 6*a*)
    IV.   Objection (vv. 6*b*-7)
     V.   Reassurance (vv. 8-11)

The divine confrontation between the prophet and God does not take place while he is tending sheep (Moses) or grinding grain (Gideon). Instead it would appear that the prophet overhears a conversation in heaven. It is a conversation between heavenly beings who are talking about God. Note the references to God in the third person. Then, one of the divine beings directs a specific introductory word to the prophet ("A voice cries out . . . ") to announce an unbelievable salvation. The prophet is commissioned to "Cry out!" this message. The objection of the prophet reflects the hopelessness and nihilism of Israel. Out of the experience of the exile he concludes that that there is nothing to say, because all humans are no more than grass, which is here today and gone tomorrow. The reassurance of the divine being begins in v. 8 with the affirmation that the word of God is not grass and that it is reliable even though grass and flowers fade. This contrast then provides the content of what the prophet must proclaim, that God's salvation cannot be evaluated simply on the basis of our present experience. Finally, there is no explicit sign in this text, at least not as we have seen them before in the calls of Moses and Gideon. One can make the argument, however, that the creation and the creative power of God to maintain it (which is described in vv. 12-26) become the sign, and that this sign is meant as a critique of Israel's religious experience at the time of the exile.

Significance. The call of Second Isaiah is a difficult text to preach to the contemporary church, because it is rooted in a theology of creation that is meant to call into question our conclusions about God that are based solely on our experience of salvation. Such experiential forms of faith are characterized as theologies of rewards and punishments. Central to the notion of a theology of reward and punishment is the belief that there is an inherent relationship between action and its outcome. This is a powerful insight about God, because it affirms the ethical nature of life. But it is also a dangerous belief.

The exile underscored one of the dangers of a theology of rewards and punishments. Israel came to believe that they lost the land because of their unfaithfulness. They concluded from the loss that they were justly punished, which meant that life was hopeless because they had become unworthy of God's salvation (40:27). The heavenly conversation in vv. 1-2 calls into question their belief, for here the prophet learns that Israel actually received double for her sins. The point of the text is not to talk about Israel's punishment, but to proclaim the impossible—a new salvation to a people who are unworthy of it. The prophet's response in vv. 6b-7 is that such a thing could never happen. By using the metaphorical language about grass withering, the prophet is reflecting on his own experience, and, on the basis of this, he concludes that humans cannot interact on a level with God. To which the divine messenger replies, Yes! (v. 8a). Agreement, however, does not end the message. Notice the disjunctive, "but" in v. 8b. The messenger then continues by stating that the word of God is more than human experience. Verse 10 goes to the heart of this message, and in so doing it provides a powerful critique of the religious experience of the prophet (and of exilic Israel). The message is that God's salvation has the power to generate its own rewards. In other words, it is a divine gift of grace that is given out according to God's own rules. Thus, even though the prophet (vv. 6b-7) and Israel (v. 27) are sure of its impossibility, the messenger proclaims in v. 11 that "[God] will feed his flock like a shepherd."

Isaiah 40 is a difficult text to preach in the contemporary church because most of our popular theology is based on our personal experiences. We frequently talk about God as savior (Jesus) or the indwelling power of the Holy Spirit (usually understood in relationship to Jesus), but we seldom explore the meaning of God as creator for our everyday life of faith. Hope in a time of hopelessness demands a strong proclamation that our savior (Jesus), whom we have all experienced in some way, is not the final word about God or about God's salvation. The way that we do this is to proclaim that the savior is also the creator, and by proclaiming this we are saying that God is more than the sum total of our religious experiences. Then faith itself becomes a critique of religious experience. Such a message provides hope when we are sure that situations are hopeless. Notice how the call of Second Isaiah does this very thing in vv. 12-26, when the messenger methodologically lists the creative power of God to measure waters, to mark off heaven, to balance hills, and so on—all aspects of God's power that the prophet has not experienced. The placement of this litany about the creator suggests that it is this unexperienced power of God that is functioning as the sign in Second Isaiah's call. This is paradoxical, however, because signs are usually themselves very experiential. The paradox is the point of the text.

The Response: *Psalm 85:1-2, 8-13*

An Oracle of Salvation

Setting. Psalm 85 follows a set liturgical pattern in which the worshiping community makes a request for God's salvation (vv. 1-7), and they then receive a divine answer in the context of their worship (vv. 8-13). The lectionary text consists of the divine answer, which was frequently given to the congregation in ancient Israel by a cultic prophet or priest in the form of a salvation oracle. Notice how the text begins in v. 8 with the speaker addressing the people by telling them that he or she is listening for a word from God.

Structure. The two-part structure of the psalm noted above could also be broken down into three parts.

> I. A Recounting of Past Salvation (vv. 1-3)
> II. A Lament and Request for a Present Salvation
> (vv. 4-7)
> III. An Oracle of Salvation (vv. 8-13)

Significance. The central theme of the lectionary psalm is a message of peace (v. 8). This peace is pictured in cosmic and holistic terms:

righteousness and peace will kiss (v. 10), heaven and earth will meet (v. 11), and God will produce a reward for the land (vv. 12-13). This final conclusion is similar to the message of reward in Isaiah 40:11.

Given the message of Isaiah 40 as a call for the prophet (and Israel) to believe in God's salvation at a time of hopelessness, you may wish to use all of Psalm 85, since the first two sections take the congregation through the act of calling on God in a time when salvation is not being experienced. This action is itself faith and thus it provides a positive response to the implied situation in Isaiah 40.

New Testament Texts

The New Testament lessons are united in their concern with the future, but they focus on different forthcoming events. The epistle lesson reflects upon "the day of the Lord"—namely, God's final judgment of creation at the end of time; and it comments on the significance of that still-future day for everyday Christian life. The Gospel text recalls John the Baptist's declared anticipation of the coming greater-one, who proves to be Jesus Christ—clearly, in the course of his historical ministry; but, in the full light of Christian faith, perhaps we may think of his promised future coming.

The Epistle: *II Peter 3:8-15a*

Living in Light of the Day of the Lord

Setting. The first part of this epistle lesson comes from a larger section (3:1-13), which deals with the "last days" and with the "day of the Lord." Through commenting on the last days in 3:1-6, II Peter moves to the idea of "the day of judgment" (3:7), which sets the stage for the initial verses of this week's reading (3:8-13). Then, vv. 14-15a complete our lesson, although they are but part of the larger unit 3:14-18. While the lectionary takes parts from two units to make the whole of the lesson, the verses cohere and make a sensible text for proclamation.

Structure. The images and language of the text are foreign to the majority of modern persons, but they were immediately intelligible to early Christians who knew the teaching, literature, and worldview of their day. Independent of the seemingly strange words and ideas of the text, the logic of the passage is quite clear. Building on the initial statement about God's disposition toward time (3:8), these verses continue by teaching about God's purposes and the future judgment

33

(3:9-10), then they elaborate and apply the teaching to life (3:11-13), and finally they exhort the readers/hearers to appropriate patterns of behavior (3:14-15).

Significance. The early Church inherited the worldview of a large part of first-century Judaism, seen in Daniel, certain apocryphal and pseudepigraphical pieces of Jewish literature, and in the Dead Sea Scrolls. That worldview was an apocalyptic outlook with a strong eschatology emphasizing God's forthcoming judgment, which would rectify the sinful condition of the world by (1) condemning and eliminating this world's order and (2) vindicating those righteous persons who remained devoted to God's will in the midst of this world's sinfulness, preserving them and bringing them into a new, sin-free creation. The Church understood that in the life, death, and resurrection of Jesus Christ, God's work of judgment had begun, and believers expected that God's work would be consummated in the "day of the Lord"—namely, the dramatic day of final judgment that would bring this world to an end.

The text expresses how one portion of the early Church dealt with the passage of time and the seeming delay of an actual end of time in a final cosmic judgment by God. It is important to recognize that the delay of the end (or, more cynically, the failure of the end to occur) did not lead II Peter to dismiss the ideas of final judgment, destruction, salvation, and new creation. Rather, the text interprets the delay and explains the relevance of the expected final judgment to life in this world prior to the end. Second Peter maintains that time has a different quality for God from what it has for humans. The finite nature of human life binds us to a chronological sense of reality, but God's eternal character sets God over time and makes time less than absolute. Second Peter continues by interpreting the seeming delay as a sign of God's graciousness, as evidence of God's desire that all humankind will repent.

Nevertheless, II Peter reiterates with confidence that God's promised judgment will transpire. The language and images of apocalyptic eschatology articulate the terrible truth of judgment, which means destruction as well as salvation. The fire of judgment was understood as a means, not merely of devastation, but especially of purification. The sinful structures of this world (cosmos!) are "dissolved" as God brings forth a new righteous creation. We should see clearly that this work of judgment, meaning purification and salvation, is God's own work. Humans experience God's work, but in the scheme of apocalyptic expectations, humans do not engineer the advent of the new creation, and they do not prompt it!

What then does all the talk of judgment mean for believers? Nothing more and nothing less than that we keep ourselves ready, that we live our lives now as we expect we shall live in God's promised new creation. Such a life is one of "peace," of experiencing the results of God's grace. And this experience of peace yields an attitude of thankfulness as we recognize the goodness of God's saving grace.

The Gospel: *Mark 1:1-8*

One Mightier Than I

Setting. Obviously this lesson comprises the opening verses of the gospel according to Mark. Older commentaries were united in their view of Mark 1:1-8 as the "prologue" to the Gospel. In turn, they referred to Mark 1:9–13:37 as the account of Jesus' ministry. But since the 1950s, interpreters have tended to view Mark 1:1-13 (some even argue for 1:1-15) as a multifaceted prologue or introduction to the Gospel. Why all this bother? How an author chooses to begin a work is often a crucial clue to comprehending the whole writing. Thus the interpretive question is "Has the story begun, or is it being 'set up'?" Fortunately, the lectionary's selection of Mark 1:1-8 gives us a portion of the text that commentators universally agree is introductory material.

Structure. Even this minimal prologue is complex. Verse 1 is practically a title for the Markan composition. Verses 2-3 are a reference to prophecy (specifically Isaiah 40:3 is quoted) declaring the early Christian conviction that John the Baptist was the forerunner of Jesus. Having explained the significance of John's activity, the prologue continues by telling of the character of John's ministry (v. 4), of the popular response to his work (v. 5), and then of John's striking appearance (v. 6). The concluding verses report the content of John's preaching. A sermon might ponder, "What is the meaning of the gospel?" And, following the text, the answers come: It is the fulfillment of God's promises; it is God's reaching out through faithful witnesses to humanity in a most striking way; it is most specifically God's work in God's Son, Jesus Christ; and it has as its focus and content the very person of Jesus.

Significance. One difficult issue related to this text about which every preacher must make a decision is whether the words *the Son of God* are an authentic part of Mark's original text. Commentaries dis-

35

cuss this problem in detail, noting the conflicting textual traditions that are equally well attested in the oldest and best manuscripts. The recent tendency to include *the Son of God,* despite the absence of the phrase in ancient and authoritative texts, is sane and defensible because of the presence of the phrase of similar words in other portions of Mark's Gospel. Moreover, the title, *Son of God,* is an accurate summary of Mark's essential understanding of Jesus; and it names the central theological theme of the Gospel. The following comments assume that *the Son of God* belongs in this passage.

A sermon cannot simply pound the point that Jesus is the Son of God. Even if we agree that the declaration is true, what exactly does it mean to say that Jesus Christ is the Son of God? Mark's whole Gospel is a deliberate effort to define the title, *Son of God.* He instructs the reader of the Gospel on the meaning of this title by playing it off against another: *Son of Man.* Through the course of the Gospel, prior to his death on the cross, only supernatural forces—God and the demons—actually recognize that Jesus is the Son of God. To all others Jesus presents himself, referring to himself steadily, as the Son of Man. We come to comprehend who Jesus Christ is as the Son of God only when we follow him through this Gospel as the Son of Man. Who then is the Son of Man? From a reading of the Gospel we can say that Jesus, the Son of Man, is the one who does God's will and God's work in battling the forces of evil for the salvation of humankind. Above all, Jesus, the Son of Man, is the one who dies on the cross, giving his life in behalf of humanity for humanity's salvation. Thus, Jesus the Son of God is God's selfless servant who gives even himself to save others! Jesus, the Son of God, makes provision for the salvation of humanity. He reveals with utter clarity the depth of God's love and the essential, selfless, serving nature of God. And Jesus, the Son of God, shows human beings the manner of life to which God calls us all.

All the wonderful and interesting information about John the Baptist in the prologue to Mark's Gospel should not lure us into major meditation on the person and the work of the Baptist. John is a forerunner, and as such he holds a high place in God's fulfillment of the promise of salvation. But John is not the Messiah. Rather he points to another, greater than he, who is both the focus of our attention in this Gospel, and, as believers, the object of our devotion. It is Jesus Christ who issues the baptism in the Holy Spirit—namely, the power and presence of the saving grace of God. As we know him, we know God and we come to understand ourselves. Through Jesus Christ we come to have a christo-logically focused theology that has sufficient content and precision to allow us, in turn—but, only in turn—to develop a theological under-standing of human nature and behavior.

ADVENT 2: THE CELEBRATION

"Preparing" is a key concept which appears in all of today's lessons. While waiting (last Sunday's theme) we are actively engaged in prepar-ing for the appearance of the Savior as we anticipate both the historical consummation at the end of time and the anamnesis of the nativity at Bethlehem. (Remember that homiletically and liturgically anamnesis is the dynamic remembering or recalling of the events of salvation in such a way that by the power of the Spirit those events are made present to the participants.) The role of John the Baptist models a type of prepara-tion for us—that of proclamation. We who wait between the times are called to a ministry of witness to Christ who is the beginning and the end and in whom all things hold together. This proclamation inevitably involves a call to repent (Mark 1:4), to get our lives straightened out (Mark 1:3), and to embrace peace as the characterization of our com-mon life (II Peter 3:14).

The hymn "On Jordan's Bank the Baptist's Cry" is particularly appropriate for this day. Notice that the third stanza (in many hymnals) picks up an image from the Old Testament lesson: "without thy grace we waste away/like flowers that wither and decay." This can make the hymn an effective bridge between the two lessons (if the epistle is omitted). The first three stanzas could be sung between the lessons and the last two in response to the reading of the Gospel. Or the entire hymn could be a response to the Gospel or the sermon. Some hymnals which include the third stanza are *The Hymnal* 1982 (Episcopal), the *Lutheran Book of Worship,* the *United Methodist Supplement to the Book of Hymns, the UCC Hymnal,* and *Worship II: A Hymnal for Roman Catholic Parishes.* The text is not under copyright. Winchester New is an easy and singable tune for it.

Also related to both the Isaiah and Mark lessons is the hymn "There's a Voice in the Wilderness Crying." It can be adapted for choirs or a solo voice. Versions of it are found in *The Hymnal* 1982, the *United Methodist Book of Hymns* (1964), and the *UCC Hymnal.*

"Prepare Ye the Way of the Lord" from Godspell provides a dynamic introit for this day.

The Isaiah lesson, with its shepherd image, allows for the use of "Savior Like a Shepherd Lead Us" as another possible hymn of response.

For congregations that use sung antiphons or responses as part of the psalter, it should be noted that the response in *The United Methodist Hymnal* is from the Isaiah lesson, thus binding lesson and psalm together in an obvious way. The chorus to the gospel hymn "Revive Us Again" will also serve as a sung response to the psalm, reflecting as it does v. 6. Text and music can be found in many of the standard gospel hymnbooks and in *Hymns for the Family of God* (Nashville: Paragon, 1976).

Third Sunday of Advent

Old Testament Texts

Isaiah 61 incorporates features of a prophetic call to Israel at a time of suffering, while Psalm 126 is a call for salvation.

The Lesson: *Isaiah 61:1-4, 8-11*

A Prophetic Anointing

Setting. Isaiah 61 is a puzzling text because the opening verses of the chapter pick up many of the motifs of the servants songs (Isaiah 42:1-4; 49:1-6; 50:4-11; 52:13–53:12—for discussion see Year A, First Sunday After Epiphany). Especially noteworthy in this case is the way in which the prophet describes being filled with the spirit of God (61:1). Yet the chapter does not identify the prophet as the "servant of God" as happens in the four servant songs, which cautions the reader about making a too easy identification. Furthermore, the servant songs do not describe the prophetic call with the monarchical imagery of being "anointed," as is the case in 61:1. These similarities and differences have prompted scholars to speculate that perhaps Isaiah 61:1-3 is the call of yet another prophet in the tradition of Isaiah who is addressing Israel in the post-exilic period, rather than in the exilic period as was the case with Second Isaiah, or the pre-exilic period as was the case with First Isaiah. Thus the book of Isaiah may consist of three different prophetic voices, and our text might be the call of the third voice (Third Isaiah). Isaiah 61 would suggest that Third Isaiah is building on the language of Second Isaiah (imagery of being spirit filled), but also making significant changes by not identifying himself as the servant and by picking up the royal imagery of anointing to describe the prophetic call. What is important for preaching this text is not whether this is the call of Third Isaiah, but that we realize aspects of the genre of a prophetic call in the construction of the text.

Structure. Isaiah 61 separates into three parts.

  I. The Call of the Prophet and Its Results (vv. 1-7)
    A. The call of the prophet (vv. 1-3*a*)
    B. The results of the prophet's message (vv. 3*b*-7)
      1. Israel will be called righteous (vv. 3*b*-5)
      2. Israel will be priests of God (vv. 6-7)
  II. A Divine Oracle and Its Results (vv. 8-9)
    A. The divine oracle (v. 8)
    B. The results of the divine oracle (v. 9)
  III. A Concluding Hymn of Praise and Its Results
    (vv. 10-11)
    A. The prophet's praise to God (v. 10)
    B. The results (v. 11)

The structure of Isaiah 61 is difficult to determine because of textual problems with the Hebrew text (e.g., v. 7*b*) and the variety of different genres that are interwoven (e.g., prophetic call, divine oracle, hymn). The present structure has been determined by noting that the prophet is the speaker at the beginning (vv. 1-7) and at the end of the chapter (vv. 10-11), while the center consists of a divine oracle (vv. 8-9). Within this three-part structure it also appears that each section is divided between an initial declaration—either about a call, a divine oracle of salvation, or a hymn of praise—and the future result of each of these actions.

Significance. Several clues allow us to sketch the context of this text as one of suffering. Those addressed by the prophet are the oppressed, the captives, the prisoners, as well as those who mourn and presently have a weak spirit (vv. 1-3). Furthermore, the situation of the audience consists of ancient ruins and devastated cities (v. 4). The three sections of the text must be read with this as background.

The call of the prophet (vv. 1-3*a*) and its results (vv. 3*b*-7): Verse 1 makes it clear that the spirit-filled anointing results in the prophet being "sent out." A series of seven infinitives follow to fill out the task of the prophet, which includes: to announce, to bind up, to call, to call, to comfort, to place, and to give. The verb "to call or proclaim" (Hebrew, *qr'*) stands out because it is used at the center of the list of verbs and repeated. The repetition underscores the two-part focus of the prophet's message. One aim is to proclaim liberation to humans ("to proclaim liberty to the captives and release to the prisoners," v. 1b). The other aim provides the reason for the liberation, which is the proclamation of a new order to creation ("to proclaim the year of the LORD's favor, and the day of vengeance of our God"). The imagery in this two-part proclamation builds upon the Jubilee legislation (Leviticus 25), where all debts were forgiven every fiftieth year.

The prophet's call is to proclaim the imminence of this time of salvation, which may very well have taken on eschatological significance in our text, with the result that the Jubilee year signifies a whole new order to creation. The closing line of the prophet's call underscores the character of the new age of salvation with a metaphor of reversal in which ashes are replaced with a garland or headdress (Hebrew, $p'r$). The verb "to proclaim" in v. 3b (Hebrew, qr') marks the transition from the prophet's call to its results. There are two results to the proclamation of a new salvation. One for Israel and the other for the nations. The result for Israel is that they "will be called oaks of righteousness, the planting of the LORD, to display his glory." The closing line, "to display his glory," plays off the "headdress" that was given to Israel in v. 3b, since in Hebrew this phrase is built from the same root word as garland (Hebrew, $p'r$). The play on the word would suggest that to receive a headdress from God results in radiating that quality to others. Salvation is two-sided, however, and while Israel radiates the glory of God, others will by definition stand outside (vv. 5-7, these verses have not been included in the lectionary, but clearly participate in the larger structure of the text). The separation of Israel and others is not the end of the text.

The divine oracle (v. 8) and its results (v. 9): The prophetic proclamation gives way to a divine oracle of salvation, in which God's character is defined as loving justice and hating robbery, which then provides the basis for promises of covenant. The result of the divine oracle of salvation parallels the role of Israel in the opening section, since, once again, the gift of divine salvation will affect Israel's interaction with the nations. The nations will take notice and even investigate Israel because of God's blessing.

The hymn of praise (v. 10) and its results (v. 11): The future promises of the first two sections take on present significance in the closing hymn when the prophet moves from proclamation to praise. Verse 10 affirms the present salvation of God in the life of the prophet ("for he [God] has clothed me with the garments of salvation, he has covered me with the robe of righteousness"). This reality is sketched out with the metaphor of the headdress (Hebrew, *p'r*) that was a future hope in the opening section. The result of the prophet's present salvation (e.g., the headdress) is a future hope that this salvation will one day be extended to all nations (v. 11).

Isaiah 61 is ultimately a text about the future. The goal of salvation is not simply the salvation of the prophet (or even Israel), but a new world order. The chapter ends with the Year of Jubilee not yet being realized. In view of this situation Isaiah 61 provides detailed guidelines concerning how we live the life of faith during Advent. It provides two particular focuses for preaching. One, the prophetic hymn underscores how our experience of salvation must not be mistaken for the completion of God's aims in this world. Even though the prophet is already clothed in God's salvation, his song ends by looking to a bigger future. Second, the shift in each section of the text (from a proclamation of salvation to its results) is a strong message of how salvation (e.g., receiving God's headdress) demands mission (e.g., displaying God's glory).

The Response: *Psalm 126*

Daring to Dream

Setting. Psalm 126 is part of a larger collection (Psalm 120–134) entitled the Psalms of Ascent. Scholars disagree about what is meant by Ascent. Although no clear single answer has been given, one of the more probable answers is that Psalms of Ascent are pilgrimage songs, used by those who journeyed to the Temple in Jerusalem. This image is particularly appropriate for Advent, since it is a season in which we are conscious about being on a journey toward Christmas to which we have not yet arrived. Psalm 126 is a national lament. As such it would be a psalm that explored how God's salvation was distant during the journey.

Structure. The psalm separates into two parts. Verses 1-3 recount God's past salvation. The historical reference here is probably to the return from exile in the sixth century B.C.E. Verses 4-6 change the focus from the celebration of a past salvation to the request for a new one. Its opening words are a plea: "Restore our fortunes, O LORD."

Significance. The psalm presents a powerful image in v. 1 that explores a central characteristic of faith during Advent. It is the image of salvation as a dream. The restoration of Zion was more than anyone had hoped. Being part of the return was like being in a dreamlike state.

The point of the psalm, however, is not to dwell on the fulfillment of past dreams, but to have the courage of faith to request that God produce new ones. Living the life of faith during Advent is daring to dream about the future.

New Testament Texts

The texts have a relationship similar to that between those for last week. The benediction in relation to "the coming of our Lord Jesus Christ" in I Thessalonians 5:23 suggests this section of the letter as an Advent text. The Gospel lesson, however, is again concerned with the appearance of Jesus Christ in his historical ministry rather than with his triumphant end-time coming.

The Epistle: *I Thessalonians 5:16-24*

Living in the Light of God's Faithfulness

Setting. I Thessalonians is likely the earliest preserved Pauline letter, and as such, it is likely the earliest preserved piece of Christian literature. Paul writes from Corinth to address issues and concerns in the life of the Thessalonian congregation. In a nutshell, the members of the church suffer persecution by non-believers. Exactly what afflictions were experienced by the Thessalonians is not clear, but Paul writes to confirm and direct them in their faith.

The verses of this week's lesson come from both the last parenetic section of the letter and from its closing. In the body of the letter Paul and his colleagues have addressed the issues of Christian suffering and even death, examining both in the light of the promised coming of the Lord Jesus Christ. Having called the Thessalonians to a life-style of mutual support, the letter moves toward its conclusion by issuing pointed instructions, vv. 12-22, and pronouncing a benediction, vv. 23-24.

Structure. The lesson falls into two broad parts, vv. 16-22 (parenesis) and vv. 23-24 (benediction). There is, however, a discernible structure in these verses that may be instructive for shaping the sermon: Verses 16-22 make eight imperative declarations. There are three positive commands—rejoice, pray, and give thanks—which are activities said to be the will of God. Then, there are two prohibitions—do not quench the Spirit and do not despise prophecy. Rather than to do these two forbidden things, the Thessalonians are told to do three positive acts—test everything, hold to what is good, and avoid every sort of evil. In turn, the benediction utters a prayer to God for the peace and sanctity of the congregation, and, then, it promises that God who called the Thessalonians is faithful and will achieve their peace and sanctity.

Significance. The combination of Paul's somewhat detailed parenesis and the words of the benediction make a powerful text for Christian proclamation. Though the benediction follows the directions given to the Thessalonians in vv. 16-22, the benediction (vv. 23-24) is the key to understanding the dynamics of Christian life as they are prescribed in the parenesis. Paul's prayer-wish ("May the God of peace . . . the coming of our Lord Jesus Christ") and his promise ("The one who calls you is faithful . . . he will do this") appeal to and declare the source of power for our lives as believers in this world—namely, God. God is source, basis, and guarantee of the life of Christian faith. We are not merely called and told to "be good," rather we are reminded—or, better, reassured—that God is the one who calls, challenges, changes, and completes our lives, bringing us into the kind of existence that he intends for us.

Yet, as the instructions preceding the benediction make clear, Christian life is not passive magic. We participate in God's grace. We experience it in growth; we express it in worship; we may even resist God's grace and, perhaps inadvertently, thwart or subvert God's goodness. Thus, Paul calls the Thessalonians, and the text calls us, to positive action. We are to orient our lives toward God, seeking God's will in prayer; and as we benefit from God's will being actualized in our lives, we are to well up in worshipful joy and thanksgiving. A devout life is essential for the operation of God's grace to be fully effective among us, though we must ever remind ourselves that we experience grace because God is at work, not because we inaugurate or permit God's efforts. As our lives are oriented toward God, we will know God's presence and power among us, and we will perceive, with increasing clarity, God's purposes.

Piety has acquired a bad name in the late-twentieth century. It is taken for a holier-than-thou disposition or for a disengagement from reality; and this is not surprising in a world where basketball players cross themselves before taking foul shots and boxers fall to their knees in the ring before slugging it out with one another. But notice that this text cuts against the quick dismissal of piety. As this passage shows, true piety is robust devotion to God that grounds and guides our existence in God's ways. God's faithfulness draws us toward God in wor-

ship and gives us a perspective for evaluating the validity of the many
claims made on our lives by the complex world in which we live.

The Gospel: *John 1:6-8, 19-28*

Knowing God, Christ, and Self

Setting. The first eighteen verses of the gospel according to John are
often called the prologue to the Gospel, for they function as a kind of
frontispiece to the writing. Following the prologue to the Gospel, John
1:19-34 is a two-part testimony from John the Baptist. After these
"introductory" materials, we come to the account of the ministry of
Jesus, which begins with the story of the calling of the disciples.

Structure. The prologue (1:1-18) is formed, as is much of the rest of
the Gospel, by a rich combination of historical reporting about John the
Baptist (1:6-7, 15), poetic expression about the person and work of Jesus
Christ (1:1-5, 10-12*a*, 14, 16), and narrative commentary (1:8-9, 12*b*-13,
17-18). Following the prologue, John 1:19-34 is a two-part testimony
from the Baptist. First, he gives witness before the representatives of the
priests and Levites in 1:19-28, an essentially negative passage where
John denies any messianic identity for himself and minimizes his own
importance in comparison with the one coming after him. Then, in 1:29-
34 John sees Jesus and gives a positive witness that confirms his identity
as the Spirit-anointed, elect Lamb of God who takes away the sin of the
world. Our lesson draws on portions of the historical reporting (1:6-7),
the narrative commentary (1:8), and the Baptist's testimony (1:19-28).
Creative preachers may note and work with the different tones, points of
view, and intentions of these materials.

Significance. The Fourth Gospel presents John the Baptist as one sent
from God. He came into the world which was, as the Gospel tells us, "in
darkness," to testify to the light that was coming into the gloom. John the
Baptist's appearance in history interrupted the course of events, much as
these prosaic verses interrupt the poetic meditation on the Incarnation of
the Word—in preparation for the forthcoming appearance of Jesus in the
Gospel's narrative. Although John is cast here in an inferior role, as a
forerunner, he is held high in the view of the prologue as the divinely-
appointed and divinely-sent witness to Jesus Christ. The text, however,
has as its main concern, not John, but God's work in Jesus Christ. This
text is profoundly theological. It sets darkness against light, and it maintains that God prepared for the appearance of light in the darkness. God's

deliberateness is crucial, indeed revelatory, for it is only because of the testimony to the light and the appearance of the light that we are able to know that ours is a condition of darkness. God saw in the dark when humanity was night-blind.

The second set of verses in this Gospel lesson record John's first words of witness to the one who was to come after him. The text shows us what it means to "know thyself" in relation to Jesus Christ. First, in his pattern of denials, John the Baptist demonstrates that in relation to Christ, faithful servants of God do not live with illusions of grandeur. As we come under the active will of God, as we live faithfully in keeping with God's will, we know who we are not! We are not the savior(s) of the world. Knowledge of God's will at work in Christ gives meaning to life that sets us free from shouldering the load for the salvation of the world. John is freed from a sense of false identity! Second, John not only knows who he isn't, as he fulfills his God-given commission he also knows who he is. Our lives take on identity, purpose, direction, conviction, and courage as we live out God's will. As we know God's will for our lives and do it, we know who we are. Gone is the debilitating adolescent crisis of identity, Who am I? As we know God's will and work in Christ, we are assured of who we are. Third, knowing Christ gives us certitude for life. As John looked beyond his own efforts to the saving work of Jesus Christ, he found genuine humility that obviously gave him strength and courage for faithful living. Because he looked to one "above" him, John dared to declare God's will and to call others to baptism. Our world steadily seeks to lure us into self-absorption, self-satisfaction, and self-actualization. In this world, a religious sense of unworthiness is equated with a bad self-image. Popular thinking contends that religious humility is a complex from which we need to be liberated. But look at the Baptist! Far from self-absorption, his sense of humility in relation to Christ eventuated in a courageous life of service that was free from the genuine oppression of sheer self-centeredness. God's commission and Christ's holiness are our greatest hope for meaningful existence! In relation to Jesus Christ we are freed from illusions, given a clear sense of identity, and strengthened for genuine service to God and humankind.

ADVENT 3: THE CELEBRATION

Today is Gaudete Sunday, from the opening word, "Rejoice," in the Latin introit (Philippians 4:4). It is the church's recognition that the

Christmas celebration is very near. This is the day for the use of the rose candle in the Advent wreath, if one is used at all (see commentary on p. 15). The Old Testament lesson for today can also provide the introit or responsive call to worship in keeping with the Gaudete theme, as follows:

> I will greatly rejoice in the Lord:
> **my whole being shall exult in my God,**
> who has clothed me with the garments of salvation,
> **who has covered me with the robe of righteousness.**

The earlier part of Isaiah 61 is reflected in the hymn, "Hail to the Lord's Anointed."

An alternative antiphon verse to be used with Psalm 126 might be the line from the gospel hymn, "We shall come rejoicing, bringing in the sheaves." If the psalm is read responsively, the line could be sung at the beginning, between vv. 3 and 4, and at the end.

It should be observed that I Thessalonians 5:16-18a, 23 will serve as a dismissal and blessing for this day. The "Rejoice" theme is thus carried from the opening act of the worship to the closing. The last stanza of "Rejoice, the Lord Is King" is a fitting choral or congregational response. Because it is not included in all hymnals, we print it here.

> Rejoice in glorious hope;
>   Jesus the Judge shall come,
> And take his servants up
>   To their eternal home:
>   We soon shall hear th' archangel's voice;
>   The trump of God shall sound: Rejoice!

Today's Gospel casts an antidotal or contrasting shadow upon the theme of rejoicing with John the Baptist's solemn warning that "Among you stands one whom you do not know." In the midst of the Christmas rush—as we brush hurriedly by folks to get the shopping done, to tend to all the details of our private lives, and to get our rejoicing in order—do we miss the One in whose name it is done? St. Irenaeus has a suggestive commentary on what is involved in seeing God in our midst. (The translation has been altered slightly to make it more inclusive to contemporary ears.)

We do not see God by our own powers; but when God pleases He is seen by us, by whom He wills, and when He wills, and as He wills. For God is powerful in all things, having been seen at that time indeed, prophetically through the Spirit, and seen, too, adoptively through the Son; and He shall also be seen paternally in the kingdom of heaven, the Spirit truly preparing us in the Son of God, and the Son leading us to the Father, while the Father, too, confers [upon us] incorruption for eternal life, which comes to every one from the fact of our seeing God. For as those who see the light are within the light, and partake of its brilliancy; even so, those who see God are in God, and receive of His splendour. But [God's] splendour vivifies them; those, therefore, who see God, do receive life. And for this reason, [God, although] beyond comprehension, and boundless and invisible, rendered Himself visible, and comprehensible, and within the capacity of those who believe, that He might vivify those who receive and behold Him through faith. For as His greatness is past finding out, so also His goodness is beyond expression; by which having been seen, He bestows life upon those who see Him. It is not possible to live apart from life, and the means of life is found in fellowship with God; but fellowship with God is to know God, and to enjoy His goodness. (St. Irenaeus, Against Heresies, IV.20.5 in Roberts and Donaldson, ed., The Ante-Nicene Fathers—Vol. 1 [New York: Scribner's, 1905], p. 489)

Fourth Sunday of Advent

Old Testament Texts

Second Samuel 7 begins by recounting how David desired to build God a temple. But in midstream the text goes through a reversal when God informs David that he would build him a house. This promise lays the groundwork for exposing a theology of election. Luke 1:47-55 is the Magnificat, in which Mary gives thanks for her pregnancy.

The Lesson: *II Samuel 7:1-11, 16*

A Promise with a Twist

Setting. Second Samuel 7 is a well-known text. It is the narrative that establishes God's unconditional promise to David that a member of his house would rule Israel forever. This promise is the starting point of messianic theology in ancient Israel. It is central to Christianity because Jesus is confessed to be the fulfillment of the messianic promise to David. This text has assumed a central role in Christian tradition, but we do not read it very closely once we have made the connection between the messianic promise to David and Jesus. The text certainly presents the messianic ideal, but it does it with a twist.

Structure. Second Samuel 7:1-11, 16 separates into two parts.

> I. David's Plan to Build God a House (vv. 1-3)
> II. God's Response (vv. 4-11, 16)
>   A. The first speech (vv. 4-7)
>   B. The second speech (vv. 8-11, 16)

Significance. Second Samuel 7 appears on the surface to be such a simple narrative. Yet when we look at the motifs and characters that enter these few verses nothing could be further from the truth. This is a complex story that includes most of the major symbols and problems of ancient Israelite faith: king, prophet, ark, temple, blindness (pious motivation to do something for God and prophetic approval that in fact does not represent God's wishes), revelation, power, and election. How do all of these motifs interrelate?

The beginning of the story is important. It opens with David, who is not named but, instead, is described only with the title, "the king." The use of this title twice in vv. 1-3 is a red flag. The larger story of the rise of the monarchy (Joshua, Judges, Samuel, Kings) makes it clear that the installation of a king in Israel presents a variety of religious problems. The central problem is stated in I Samuel 8:6-9, when Israel requests a king for protection against the Philistines, and God informs Samuel that such a request is not a rejection of Samuel, but of God as king. We learn a number of things about the king in vv. 1-3: He is dwelling in a house, God has given him peace, he desires the ark of God also to be in a house, and his piety is sincere (the prophet tells us as much with the closing remark, "The Lord is with you"). The last point is very important. Piety permeates the opening verses. The king's intentions appear to be pure, which prompts (the somewhat unusual) immediate prophetic agreement that the king should build God a temple. Yet this is the dangerous aspect of the story, because housing the ark (the central symbol of the God of the exodus) in a permanent temple has implications that go beyond the pious intentions of the king. Kings and temples frequently go together in the ancient Near East to create a civil religion in which the king is viewed as nearly divine, or at the very least as God's primary representative on earth. In such situations God and state become so intermingled precisely because of the religious and civil role of the king, which creates all kinds of problems concerning whose power is really being worshiped.

Although the topic of conversation between king and prophet has been religious, it is important to note that God has actually been absent from the opening scene. When God does enter at v. 4, however, he virtually takes over the story with two revelatory speeches that provide a response to the pious intentions of king and prophet. The introduction of formal categories of revelation to the prophet Nathan ("Thus says the Lord . . . ") underscores the absence of divine inquiry in the opening section. The first speech calls into question the prophet's too easy support of the king by reviewing God's past activity with Israel. The God of the Exodus is not tied to a temple and has never asked for one (vv. 6-7). The second speech focuses more explicitly on the king. Here,

God reviews David's rise to power as a divine gift (vv. 8-11*a*) and concludes this summary by reversing David's wish. Instead of David building God a house, God declares that he would build David a house.

The two parts of the story—David's wish to build God a temple and God's reversal of this wish—should not be interpreted as being in conflict, but they are in tension. It is the tension between the two parts of the story that provides an avenue for preaching this text. Our confessions of election frequently arise out of contexts that resemble the opening scene of the story. We are secure in our power and life-style, we are feeling thankful and pious about the good things that we presently experience, and in the light of this we wish to do something for God. This is what David is doing at the outset of II Samuel 7 and the prophet Nathan even agrees. God's response to David and Nathan is that they really cannot do anything for God no matter how pious their motives. In this context, the promise of election to David states just the opposite, that God has done and will continue to do tremendous things for David. The promise of election in II Samuel 7 is certainly worthy of celebration, but we must also see that in its larger context it also implies a criticism of our own sense of power and of well-being, which we too frequently mistake as the content of God's election. The story makes this point by contrasting revelation (the second part of the story) with well intended piety (the first part of the story).

The Response: *Luke 1:47-55*

A Hymn of Thanksgiving

Setting. The Magnificat ties in closely to the larger context of the New Testament lesson (Luke 1:26-38). There are two annunciations in the opening chapter of Luke (to Zechariah in 1:5-25 and to Mary in 1:26-38). The Magnificat occurs immediately after these annunciations, when Mary visits Elizabeth in 1:39. The hymn is best interpreted as a personal thanksgiving psalm.

Structure. The personal thanksgiving psalm separates into four parts. It begins with an introduction in which the singer expresses thanks to God. In the Magnificat this is v. 47. The introduction is followed by a recounting of personal experience in vv. 48-49*a*. The central motif in this section is that Mary is of low social status, and that in spite of (or because of) this God has paid close attention to her and "done great things for [her]." The third section of the thanksgiving psalm is confession. Here the singer makes declaration concerning the character of God in the light of the personal experience of salvation. Verses 49b-53 present a series of confessions about the character of God's salvation, of which the strongest element is the surprising reversals that God performs in our world: the proud are brought low and the mighty are toppled from their thrones while the lowly are lifted up. Central to the confession is an element of teaching. Mary is not only making a confession to God about the character of salvation, but also teaching fellow worshipers. The Magnificat ends on a note of confidence concerning the salvation of God. Verses 54-55 provide this concluding confidence when Mary recounts God's unconditional promise of salvation to Abraham.

Significance. The Old Testament lesson and the Magnificat can be used as complementary texts to explore the nature and power of God's salvation and the challenges that it brings to faith. The Magnificat explores the power of God's election from a very different vantage point than II Samuel 7. Rather than a king who is feeling secure on his throne, Mary is a person of low status, who is not secure in power. Thus we have two very different characters who must respond to the same unconditional promise of election. One result of these two different contexts is that the tension between David and God that was so central in the construction of II Samuel 7 is lacking in Mary's song. The lack of tension, however, should not cover over the fact that both texts explore how God's election is a surprising reversal that cannot be accounted for on the basis of our present experience alone. If the challenge for David was to see that his high social status and vast power could not be equated in any way with God's salvation, the challenge to Mary is just the reverse—to see that her low social status and seemingly powerlessness not be judged as precluding her from God's salvation.

New Testament Texts

Two elegant texts form the lessons for the Fourth Sunday of Advent. The ending of Romans is a lofty and complex doxology to God for many divine wonders, but especially the salvific work through Jesus Christ, while the passage from Luke recounts the annunciation by the angel Gabriel to Mary of the forthcoming divinely-determined birth of Jesus Christ.

The Epistle: *Romans 16:25-27*

Glory to God Through Jesus Christ, Forever!

Setting. The text is fraught with textual difficulties. Several important early manuscripts omit these verses, and still others place them
either after 14:23 or 15:33. In relation to these various readings, some
manuscripts omit v. 24 and others place it after v. 27. Today, because
of content and style, scholars generally conclude that 16:25-27 was
composed by one of Paul's associates for the use of the letter by the
larger Church in a later period. Nevertheless, this doxology recalls
Romans 1:2, 5 and provides a fitting ending to Paul's longest and most
formal composition.

Structure. The doxology is a ramble. It is actually faulty in its gram-
matical construction. From the beginning of v. 25 through the beginning
of v. 27 the text moves toward the praise of God in an extended series of
dative phrases (to God . . . to the only wise God), but with the introduction of the genitive prepositional phrase, "through Jesus Christ," the
grammar becomes derailed and the praise is finally given to Christ, perhaps indicating a lack of distinction between Christ and God in Christ!

Despite the peculiar grammar, the thought sequence is discernible,
and suggestive for preaching. The first major thought about God is that
God is able to strengthen the believers. This idea is explained in some
detail. God strengthens through the gospel, which is the proclamation
of Jesus Christ, which is the mystery kept through the ages but now dis-
closed to the Gentiles according to God's commandment for the purpose of bringing about the obedience of faith. The second accolade
toward God is that God is "only wise"—that is, the one possessing true
wisdom above all others. This thought is elaborated, again in relation to
Jesus Christ. Here, having introduced Jesus Christ as the one through
whom God accomplishes what God is about in the world, the doxology
declares the glory (specifically in relation to Jesus Christ) forever!

Significance. Inherent in the doxology are two related thoughts. God
is able (and works) to strengthen believers. Strengthening here is a
metaphor for infusing otherwise weak humans with saving power. In
other words God is attending to human deficiency, for the good of
humanity; and, indeed, God is granting a quality of life to persons who
otherwise are unable to experience the power of salvation. The saving
strengthening of God is focused in the rhetoric of this doxology specifi-

cally in relation to Jesus Christ. In fact, it is Jesus Christ who is understood to be the very revelation of the mystery of God, which was formerly obscure but now openly revealed to those outside the covenant.

We also learn from this doxology that the work of God through the good news of Jesus Christ has a specific end or purpose, namely to bring about the obedience of faith. Those who experience God's saving power are granted a new way of life. They live in compliance with the will of God because the power of God enables them to achieve God's purposes for their lives. Here is the good news: God has acted in Jesus Christ to do for humans what we cannot do for ourselves. God moves through Jesus Christ—particularly through the proclamation of the powerful love of God demonstrated in Jesus Christ—to transform human existence into a godly reality. This is the glory of God, and it is the cause of Christian celebration and praise. Moreover, what God is about in Jesus Christ has an enduring character that time will never undo, for the glory of God's salvation through Christ is glory forever!

The Gospel: *Luke 1:26-38*

Christ's Birth Foretold

Setting. The verses of the Gospel lesson follow the verses that recounted the foretelling of the birth of John the Baptist. Indeed, throughout the first two chapters of the gospel according to Luke we find an alternating series of stories, now about the Baptist and then about Jesus. The back-and-forth pattern invites us to make a comparison between John and Jesus from the time of the annunciation of their clearly special births to the time of their circumcisions, namings, and presentations. This pattern serves to establish through narrative the clear superiority of Jesus over John, and it anticipates the course and relationship of their adult ministries in Galilee.

Structure. A comparison of the annunciations of the births of John the Baptist and Jesus shows a comparable pattern at the core of the narratives. The presence and activity of the same angel, Gabriel, in both stories heightens the similarities of the accounts. Both episodes seem to follow a five-fold literary pattern established in the Old Testament for the annunciations of salvific figures: appearance of the angel, fear, delivery of a message, objection by the recipient of the visitation, and a sign offered. Yet, notably in the account of the annunciation of Jesus' birth we find elements not in keeping with the Old Testament pattern of annunciation: the (virginal) conception, the articulation of the future accomplishments of the child, and the particular elements of the portrait of Mary in vv. 34 and 38. These "special" items are noteworthy for developing a focus for preaching.

Significance. The idea of the virginal conception may be approached in a variety of ways. First, we should note the narrative relationship between 1:34-35 and 1:18-19. John the Baptist was born against the odds to old parents, Zechariah and Elizabeth, as Isaac was born to Abraham and Sarah. Clearly this is a "miraculous" birth that assumes the involvement of God. But as spectacular as are the conception and birth of John, they pale in comparison with the miracle of Jesus' own conception and birth. As God moves to bring forth the promised heir of David, he does so in a way that goes far beyond all possible human expectation. The son of Mary who is the Son of David is, above all, the divine Son, who was begotten by the Holy Spirit. At the heart of this story is the Christian conviction and claim that at a particular time and place, in a manner that supersedes the normal course of historical human events, God acted in history in relation to humankind, begetting his Son who comes in fulfillment of God's promises and for the salvation of humanity.

The child whose birth is announced by Gabriel is one whose future accomplishments also go far beyond all possible human expectations. Israel may have looked forward to the promised reestablishment of the line of David, even eternally, but there is no basis for the declaration that the child born to occupy the throne of David would (1) reign forever or (2) be the Son of God in anything other than a figurative sense. The eternal reign and the profound holiness of the child are realities beyond all human hopes! Thus the character and accomplishments of Jesus Christ are the fulfillment of God's promises demonstrating the extravagant nature of God's grace.

In this story, Mary becomes far more than a person in history or another character in another story. Her enthusiastic acceptance of God's will (despite the clear scandal that it would have caused—and suggested to first-century readers) is in sharp contrast to the cynical laughter of Sarah in the Old Testament and is closest to the response of Hannah, the mother of Samuel, in I Samuel 1:18. Indeed, the identification of Mary with Hannah prepares the reader for Mary's subsequent recitation of the Magnificat (1:46-55) with its close and pronounced parallels to Hannah's canticle in I Samuel 2:1-10. In this story Mary becomes a symbolic representative of the "poor" and faithful remnant of Israel whose piety and devotion caused them to be completely dependent on God for their well-being and, in turn, always fully accepting of God's will for their lives. Mary serves as a model of true faith, accepting God's will despite her lack of comprehension and even reservations in relation to the angelic message of God's saving work.

Taken together the various elements of this story form a message about the surprising, unforeseeable, even incomprehensible nature of God's grace. Yet the message declares that grace is real, despite its strangeness. Grace takes flesh. Grace exists in history, though it comes from beyond history's confines. Indeed, divine grace touches human existence beyond all expectations, perhaps primarily because grace itself becomes human for the genuine humanization of a hoping, but otherwise hopeless, humanity. Through divine initiative God's Spirit raises up the Son of David who achieves more than human efforts could even raise up as hope.

ADVENT 4: THE CELEBRATION

The theme of the Fourth Sunday of Advent is always the Annunciation in some form. In Year A it is the annunciation to Joseph, in Year B to Mary, and in Year C to Elizabeth. The character of Advent is preserved in these lessons because the emphasis is still on preparation; the announcement is sent today, but the party is still a few days off.

Year B provides an opportunity for the preacher to help the congregation examine the place of Mary in the whole drama of salvation. Protestant reaction to the extremes of the Marian cultus in the Middle Ages has often led to its own extreme of ignoring the scriptural witness about Mary altogether, and too little positive theologizing has been done about her role in the mystery of faith. Today's Gospel can serve to introduce some of the basic images of Mary as a model of faith, of obedience (or cooperation with the divine), and of the Church as the People of God who are called to be Christ-bearers in the world. A rather extensive literature has grown up around the Magnificat by liberation theologians, which should not be ignored but neither should some of the other biblical studies that have been fruit of the ecumenical age. A brief reading list for preachers who wish to be informed about current issues in Marian studies should begin with Chapter 8 of the Second Vatican Council's Dogmatic Constitution on the Church (Walter M. Abbott, ed., *The Documents of Vatican II* [Piscataway, N.J.: New Century,

1974], pp. 85-96). This marked a new approach in the Roman Catholic Church because it represented a conscious decision to talk about Mary within the larger realm of ecclesiology rather than in isolation. It is against the background of that document that the other books should be read. Among such volumes are Leonardo Boff, *The Maternal Face of God: The Feminine and Its Religious Expressions* (San Francisco: Harper, 1987); Raymond Brown and others, *Mary in the New Testament* (Philadelphia: Fortress, 1978); Ivone Gebara and Maria Clara Bingemer, *Mary: Mother of God, Mother of the Poor* (Maryknoll, N.Y.: Orbis, 1989); Joseph A. Grassi, *Mary, Mother and Disciple* (Wilmington, Del.: Michael Glazier, 1988); Rosemary Ruether, *Mary, the Feminine Face of the Church* (Philadelphia: Westminster, 1977); John de Satge, *Down to Earth: The New Protestant Vision of the Virgin Mary* (n.p.: Consortium, 1976).

The following is from one of the sermons of Bernard of Clairvaux (1090-1153) preached on today's Gospel:

How gracious is this union of virginity and humility! A soul in whom humility embellishes virginity and virginity ennobles humility finds no little favor with God. Imagine then how much more worthy of reverence must she have been whose humility was raised by motherhood and whose virginity consecrated by her childbearing. You are told that she is a virgin. You are told that she is humble. If you are not able to imitate the virginity of this humble maid, then imitate the humility of the virgin maid. Virginity is a praiseworthy virtue, but humility is by far the more necessary. The one is only counselled; the other is demanded. To the first you have been invited; to the second you are obliged. Concerning the first he said, "he who is able to receive this, let him receive it"; of the second is said, "Truly I said to you, unless you become like this little child, you will not enter the kingdom of heaven." The first is rewarded; the second is required. You can be saved without virginity; without humility you cannot be. Humility which deplores the loss of virginity can still find favor. Yet I dare say that without humility not even Mary's virginity would have been acceptable. The Lord says, "Upon whom shall my Spirit rest, if not upon him that is humble and contrite in spirit?" On the humble, he says, not on the virgin. Had Mary not been humble, then, the Holy Spirit would not have rested upon her. Had he not rested upon her, she would not have become pregnant. How indeed could she have conceived by him without him? It seems evident then that she conceived by the Holy Spirit because, as she herself said, God "regarded the humility of his handmaiden" rather than her virginity. And even if it was because of her virginity that she found favor, she conceived nevertheless on account of her humility. Thus there is no doubt that her virginity was found pleasing because her humility made it so. (Bernard of Clairvaux and Amadeus of Lausanne, *Magnificat: Homilies in Praise of the Blessed Virgin Mary,* trans. Marie-Bernard Saïd and Grace Perigo [Kalamazoo: Cistercian Publications, 1979], pp. 9-10)

The hymn "Of the Father's Love Begotten" is particularly appropriate today. Metrical versions of the Magnificat appear in the recent editions of several denominational hymnals. "Hail to the Lord's Anointed" is suggested by the Old Testament lesson.

The Nicene Creed, with its affirmation that Jesus "was incarnate of the Holy Spirit and the Virgin Mary," will echo the witness of the Gospel.

THE PASCHAL MYSTERY AND CHRISTMAS/EPIPHANY

Those who were trained in the old "pie chart" understanding of the Christian year may be a bit surprised to discover that the new calendar speaks of Christmas/Epiphany, with January 6 being the last day of Christmas, rather than the first day of a new season. The reason for this change is actually a return to the origins of both festivals, Christmas and Epiphany, and a recognition that the division of the two into separate seasons was really the result of Western chauvinism. Epiphany, the older of the two festivals, originated in the East, and celebrated both the birth and the baptism of Jesus. It also emphasized the mystery of the Incarnation as central to understanding these events. Christmas, as a feast of the nativity in particular, developed later in Rome. Some have maintained that December 25 was chosen to compete with the cult of Mithra, which celebrated the birth of its sun god on that day. Others suggest more complicated reasons having to do with dating back from what was believed to have been the date of the crucifixion.

December 25 won out in the Western church as the date for celebrating the birth of Jesus. Because January 6 had been so important earlier, it was retained, but the emphasis on Epiphany, the manifestation of God in the world, was reduced to the visit of the wise men, who were pictured as being of three races, so as to symbolize the whole world. The races were rarely ever pictured as including Caucasians, giving the impression that only "colored peoples" were in need of missionary outreach! In American Protestantism, this was to become the rationale for turning the season of Epiphany into a programmatic occasion emphasizing missions. Visiting missionaries combed the countrysides during the worst weather of the year in faithfulness to the pie chart, and confirmation classes were taught that green was the color of the season because it symbolized the growth of the church through missionary activity! The difficulty with this approach is not so much that it is misleading, but that it is so limited in its understanding of mission. The church's mission grows not out of the visit of the magi, but out of the whole work of Christ, and therefore mission is an appropriate topic at anytime, because it is the reason for the church's existence. The Western church's particular emphasis also led to an eclipse of the baptism of Jesus and its commemoration.

To counter some of this misunderstanding the new calendar observes a festival of the Incarnation and Manifestation from December 25 through January 6, Christmas through Epiphany. It then observes time "after Epiphany," or, in some traditions, "ordinary time." The First Sunday After Epiphany is the Baptism of the Lord, thus bringing that event into prominence once more.

Another difficulty with referring to the visit of the Magi as "the Epiphany" in such an exclusive way is that it ignores the fact that the Gospels are rich in epiphanies. The intent of the Gospels is to be an epiphany by recording "all that Jesus began to do and to teach." Having celebrated the birth of Jesus at Christmas/Epiphany, the time after Epiphany is spent examining who this is who has come among us. Each year the last Sunday after Epiphany, regardless of how many Sundays there may be, is the Sunday of the Transfiguration. This is the epiphany that begins the chain of events leading to Jesus' death and resurrection.

So it is the Paschal mystery that finally enables us to interpret Christmas and Epiphany. The Gospel writers constantly report the amazement or lack of comprehension that accompanies Jesus' ministry; understanding only comes by the light of the resurrection. As we do not celebrate Advent by pretending Christ has not come, so we do not celebrate Christmas by pretending we don't know what is going to happen to this child. Christmas cannot be celebrated properly in isolation from the rest of the Christ-event. To separate the story of Jesus' birth from the harsh reality of the crucifixion is to engage in a pious fraud, a sentimental blasphemy. Careful exegesis of the lessons for the time will make evident the opportunities the Scripture gives to relate incarnation and atonement, the cradle and the cross.

Because Epiphany day will usually fall during the week, the lectionary gives the option of substituting it and its lessons on the First Sunday After Christmas. Provided January 6 falls later than the Second Sunday After Christmas it could also be observed on that day. The reason for this is that the First Sunday After Epiphany is always the Baptism of the Lord, thus giving priority to an event that is attested to by all the Gospels. Because of space limitations, commentary on the Second Sunday After Christmas (whose propers never vary) may be found in the first volume of the Year A series.

The Services of Christmas

The Western Catholic tradition has observed three services for Christmas Day: one at midnight, one at dawn, and one during the day. That accounts for the three propers listed in the lectionary. Because of space, this series will deal with one proper each year. The lessons remain the same for all three years, and worship planners may exercise the option of changing the lessons around between the services. This is encouraged in the case of the Gospel reading for the service during the day, the Johannine prologue, if there is a chance that it will be omitted otherwise. For those who wish to use John 1 this year, see the exegetical comment in the first volume of the Year A series, where it also appears as the Gospel reading for the Second Sunday After Christmas.

The pattern in much of American Protestantism is to have one or two earlier services followed by a midnight service on Christmas Eve, and only in rare instances are services held on Christmas Day at all. Usually the earlier service is a "family" or "children's" service. The set of three propers in the lectionary can be adapted very easily to this tradition, particularly since the Gospel reading for the first two propers are the familiar Christmas story from Luke.

If there is a crèche in the church, the placing of the figure of Jesus in the manger might take place after the reading of Luke 2:7. This could be accompanied by the singing of one or more stanzas of "Away in a Manger," and the use of the following unison prayer:

> Lord Jesus,
> I offer to you
> the gold of my love,
> the incense of my prayers,
> the myrrh of my willingness to bear the cross.
> Amen.

The service would then continue with the reading of the Gospel. For those who object to such an interruption of the Gospel reading, this brief devotion can be used as an entrance rite at the beginning of the service, with the image of Jesus being brought in during the procession.

Christmas is a popular time for "candlelight services," and they are often advertised in such a way as to give the impression that the candlelight is an end in itself rather than a rich symbol of what the birth of Christ means to the world. Attention to the Paschal character of our worship will always help us guard against a manipulated sentimental religiosity. Ideally, the Advent wreath, with its function of "counting down" to Christmas, should disappear before the first service of the season. If it has come equipped with a "Christ candle," light only that candle for these services of Christmas Eve/Day. After that it should vanish, so as not to give the impression that it is on an equal footing with the Paschal candle, which is the primary light in the church symbolizing the presence of Christ. Again, it is the Paschal symbol that takes priority and gives meaning to what we are doing, even at Christmas.

Where the service involves all the members of the congregation having lighted candles, take care that directions are clear, brief, and to the point. The effect of the occasion is diminished if the pastor is giving warnings about dropping wax on the new carpet! Imaginative worship planners should think about how a service can be a "candlelight" service without having to put live flames in the hands of everyone present.

The midnight service is most appropriately eucharistic, and that emphasis should not be overshadowed by any candlelighting exercise, a case of bad liturgy driving out good. Christmas is the celebration of the Incarnation, the scandalous proclamation that God took on human flesh and blood. The elements of bread and wine remind us of this "materialistic" character of God who comes to meet us again in the Eucharist, a symbol of Christ incarnate.

Just as the services of Advent have been characterized by reserve and a sense of anticipation, so the services of Christmas unleash a torrent of praise and adoration through word, music, and visuals. Avoid clutter in both chancel and nave to allow for adequate liturgical movement. If live Christmas trees are used, let them be in proportion to the space, and, hopefully, potted, so that later they can be planted as a sign of ecological responsibility. Give some thought as to whether they are decorated or left bare. Candles and flowers should point to the Lord's Table, neither camouflaging it nor making it difficult to set for the Eucharist. The church's celebratory colors of white and/or gold are used during this time.

Christmas Day, Second Proper

Old Testament Texts

Isaiah 62:6-12 provides an eschatological vision of Zion, while Psalm 97 is a celebration of God's future rule in Zion.

The Lesson: *Isaiah 62:6-12*

Calling God to Account for Promises

Setting. Isaiah 62:6-12 is part of a larger unit of literature that spans Isaiah 60–62. A brief outline of this section of poetry will aid us in interpreting four lectionary texts in this volume (61:1-4, 8-11 for the Third Sunday of Advent, 62:6-12 for Christmas, 61:10–62:3 for the First Sunday After Christmas Day, 60:1-6 for Epiphany). Commentators suggest that Isaiah 60–62 separates into three parts by chapters and that each of these three chapters divides into a lament and a word of salvation to counter the lament. The aspect of lament arises in these chapters because the historical situation to which the prophet is speaking does not correspond to the vision of salvation that is being described. These visions of salvation, therefore, are eschatological. In spite of the modest tension between the present and the future, a future vision of salvation dominates the laments. We might outline the three chapters in the following manner under the heading, "A Proclamation of Salvation."

I. The Nations Will Worship at Zion (60)
   (Epiphany, 61:1-6)
II. The Anointing of a Prophet-Mediator (61)
   (Third Sunday of Advent, 61:1-4, 8-11;
   First Sunday After Christmas Day, 61:10–62:3)
III. The Renewal of Zion (62)
   (Christmas, 62:6-12)

Structure. Isaiah 62 separates into two parts that combine to describe the renewal of Zion.

I. Zion Is Renamed (vv. 1-5)
II. Zion Is Restored (vv. 6-12)

The lectionary text includes the second half of Isaiah 62. The description of the complete restoration of salvation in Zion may be limited to vv. 6-9, with vv. 10-12 providing an ending to the larger unit of Isaiah 60–62. Note how vv. 10-12 incorporate much of the language of Second Isaiah's call (40:1-11, especially the reference to a highway and the affirmation that God's salvation brings its own reward). These quotations have prompted scholars to suggest that Isaiah 60–62 is the core message of a later post-exilic prophet (Third Isaiah), who has taken the message of an imminent act of salvation from Second Isaiah (e.g., the return from exile) and refashioned it into an eschatological vision of a future state of salvation (e.g., the restoration of Zion at the end of time).

Significance. The central issue for preaching this text is to determine who is speaking. Who is the "I" in v. 6? There are two choices and, as you might imagine, scholars are divided. One possibility is to identify the "I" as God, while the other possibility is to identify the "I" as the prophet. In order to answer this question the larger context of Isaiah 62 must be taken into account, since the "I" also occurs in v. 1. An overview of the text would suggest that the prophet is the speaker. Note the frequent third person reference to God or to the Lord in vv. 3, 5, 6.

Once it is granted that the "I" of v. 6 is the prophet, then Isaiah 62:6-7 is not just an oracle of salvation. Rather it presents a picture of the prophet calling God to account for the fact that the salvation of Zion is not yet complete. The wall of Jerusalem has been restored, but it only highlights the fact that salvation is at best partial. In view of this the prophet places watchmen (NRSV, "sentinels") on the walls of Jerusalem to badger God day and night. The Hebrew used here is *mazkir* (literally, "those who bring to remembrance"). Such persons appear to have been court officials in ancient Israel, whose function was to be the "recorder" (see II Samuel 8:16; I Kings 4:3; Isaiah 36:3). The watchmen in our text, therefore, appear to be recorders who have the written account of God's promises to Israel, and their goal is to give God no rest until the salvation begun at Jerusalem is completely realized in all the details promised by God (v. 7). Verses 8-9 provide the reason for the prophet's boldness. This section is presented as a quotation from God ("The Lord has sworn . . ."). The imagery suggests that the divine promise of salvation is being quoted back to God—perhaps by the recorders who have been summoned by the prophet. Verses 10-12 can be read as a conclusion to the smaller text as well to the larger unit, because in either case, these verses underscore the confidence of the prophet that, indeed, God will deliver on the complete promise of salvation.

Isaiah 62:6-12 provides an excellent source for preaching on Christmas, because Christmas parallels exactly the situation of this text. The Incarnation of God inaugurates a salvation that is not yet complete, not unlike the imagery in Isaiah 62:6-7 of having the walls of Jerusalem erected without the full salvation of the land being realized. The Incarnation allows Christians to badger God until the kingdom is fully realized (much like the watchmen on the Jerusalem walls), because such activity actually requires as strong a faith as that evinced by Third Isaiah.

The Response: *Psalm 97*

The Enthronement of God and the Gift of Righteousness

Setting. Psalm 97 is one of the Enthronement Psalms. This group of psalms includes 47, 93, 96, 97, 99 and is characterized by the proclamation, "Yahweh is King!" There is debate over the exact meaning of this proclamation and its cultic setting in ancient Israel. The fine points of this debate need not concern us at this time. When using this psalm for Christmas we underscore the enthronement of God in the Temple, which from a theological perspective is a celebration of divine imminence. The Incarnation of God in the birth of Jesus is also a celebration of divine imminence.

Structure. Psalm 97 separates into four parts. It begins in vv. 1-2 with a description of the enthronement of God in the Temple. Verses 3-6 describe this enthronement with the traditional imagery of theophany (e.g., clouds, darkness, fire, lightning, and the reaction of fear by nature—mountains, earth, heavens—and by people). Verses 7-9 outline the two-sided effects of God's appearing—shame and gladness. Finally, vv. 10-12 describe the relationship between God and the righteous.

Significance. Psalm 97 is a celebration of the presence of God within the worshiping community. The setting of worship underscores two points. First, the place of the theophany is not in the world, but in worship (vv. 1-7). And, second, that it is only within the context of worship that the relationship between God and the faithful ones is established (vv. 8-10). In fact, commentators define the "righteous ones" in vv. 11-12 solely by means of worship. The righteous are those who are allowed to enter the sanctuary where God has been enthroned. Thus there is an inner connection between being in the sanctuary when God is enthroned and being righteous. This conception of righteousness goes against our modern understanding of the term, which tends to be more ethical—namely, that being righteous means acting in a certain reasonable way, which may not necessarily require revelation. Righteousness in Psalm 97 is not first and foremost about action; rather it is more sacramental. It is a revelatory quality that accompanies God in the act of being enthroned ("righteousness and justice are the foundation of his throne," v. 2*b*). This quality, then, is transferred to those who are present. What this means is that the effect of theophany in the context of worship is the divine gift of righteousness. This transformation in character forces the worshiper back into the larger world as an ethical agent of God's will, because the goal of the divine enthronement is for "all the peoples [to] behold his glory" (v. 6*b*).

New Testament Texts

The texts suggest two very different meditations on God's salvation, which appeared as grace in the person of Jesus Christ.

The Epistle: *Titus 3:4-7*

Jesus Christ, God's Saving Kindness and Love

Setting. The letter to Titus is designed to give advice to a Christian leader who is facing a less than perfect pastoral situation. It gives counsel about the personal qualities a pastor is to possess, provides directions for dealing with those in the church who create problems, admonishes the pastor to teach sound doctrine, lays out standards for different types of believers, and delineates the essence of the meaning of salvation. The verses of our lesson declare the theological basis of Christian life in the present world.

Structure. Verses 4-7 are a long, single sentence in Greek. The text sets forth the essence of the gospel in a capsule form. The text has three "movements": It declares what God has done; it clarifies the cause and the medium of God's action; and it states the meaning of what God has done in relation to human beings.

Significance. The passage celebrates the goodness and loving-kind-ness of God which "has appeared" in history in the person and the work of Jesus Christ. God's work is salvation, and God achieved that new reality for humanity specifically through Jesus Christ. The reality of salvation in Christ is viewed here in terms of the experience of believ-ers, whose lives are renewed in relation to Jesus Christ. Strikingly, the personal nature of God's saving work affects the very persons of those who hold to the truth of the gospel.

Lest we misunderstand that God's salvation came in response to our human actions, the text declares that "he saved us, not because of any works of righteousness that we had done, but according to his mercy." The mercy of God is God's dealing with the human condition, and we are saved not as a reward but specifically in our unrighteousness, because God is good, loving, kind, and merciful—despite our condi-tion! This is the "good" part of the news of the gospel, that God's mercy accomplishes salvation by grace, not in terms of human merit.

The images of salvation are noteworthy: rebirth, renewal, and justifi-cation. Inherent in these images is an assumption that God's will for our lives was somehow out of line, and now God has acted to rectify our problem. Salvation sets right that which was wrong, and it sets us into the relationship with God that God intends. The gift of this divinely achieved relationship is to be appreciated, savored, and allowed to affect our existence.

As believers we live in hope with the assurance that since the work of salvation is God's, it is not restricted by the normal limitations to which we humans have become accustomed. The passage speaks of eternal life because the renewed life we now live through God's saving grace is based in God's eternal mercy and is free from the corrupting forces that once dominated our lives (see 3:3).

The Gospel: *Luke 2:(1-7) 8-20*

The Surprising Shape of Salvation

Setting. We read and preach Luke's familiar version of the story of Jesus' birth. The account is set in a highly dramatic and intensely Jewish environment, though when reading or hearing Luke's story one can never forget that the religious world of Judaism was part of a larger Greco-Roman political world. The narrative is quite deliber-ately formed, because Luke tells the story of the birth of Jesus in such

a way that the annunciation, birth, circumcision, and naming of John
the Baptist precede and alternate with the same kinds of events in the
life of Jesus. In Luke 1:5-25 the birth of John is foretold, and in Luke
1:26-38 the forthcoming birth of Jesus is announced. Then, Luke
1:57-66 tells of the birth, circumcision, and naming of John; and later,
Luke 2:1-21 narrates the birth, circumcision, and naming of Jesus.

Structure. The text for this Sunday falls naturally into three parts:
Verses 1-7 tell of the census and Jesus' birth; vv. 8-14 recount the
encounter of the shepherds and the angels; and vv. 15-20 relate the visit
of the shepherds to the holy family. One may use the text as one grand
triptych, or one may elect to select one or two of the panels for preaching
and worship. I shall discuss this passage in three distinct units.

Significance. (A) The opening verses (1-7) make a number of points.
The beginning of the section, which mentions the powers-that-were in
the Greco-Roman world, locates the holy family in the context of a
momentarily peaceful but ever politically volatile world. The mention
of Bethlehem, named as the city of David, sets the Jewish world against
the Roman-dominated political situation as it recalls the former glories
of Israel. At the same time, for one in the know, the mention of Bethlehem, the city of David, would immediately conjure up thoughts of the
promise of God to David that his heir would one day reign in peaceful
glory. The world into which Jesus was born was at peace, but it was
Caesar's peace, a human peace, and not the promised peace of God that
comes through God's gracious work, not merely human efforts.

Having conjured up shades of traditional Davidic expectations, Luke
moves to recount the birth of Jesus. He tells the story so that the humble
circumstances of Jesus' birth are accentuated. Jesus is born in a stable
and laid in a manger because there is no room for his parents (despite
Mary's obvious condition) in the normal lodging facilities; though the
world had Caesar's peace, it was still far from perfect. Despite the modest accommodations, Jesus' parents demonstrate great care by wrapping
their child neatly in the approved manner of the day. Nevertheless, one
should not forget that the conditions of the world and Joseph and Mary's
limited means preclude Jesus' birth taking place in circumstances of
great comfort. At root Luke is emphasizing the genuine humility of
Jesus' family: He was not born into power, privilege, or pleasure; instead
he arrived in plebeian surroundings adorned only with parental love.

The majestic and imaginative language of this passage invites the
responsible use of one's homiletical imagination. For example, the mention

of Jesus' being laid in the manger suggests his role as the saving food of the world (this is my body; this is my blood—for you). And the memory that there was no room for Mary, Joseph, and the babe-about-to-be in the inn foreshadows the actual reception that Jesus encountered as he lived and worked in the course of his ministry.

(B) The following verses (8-14) introduce the shepherds, who are appropriate characters, given the location in the city of David. Some scholars suggest that the shepherds were employees of the Temple, assigned to take care of the animals designated, but the precise identification of these characters is not crucial. Rather, again, Luke accentuates the humility of the situation of Jesus' birth. In Caesar's world God did not send Jesus Christ to the courts of kings, queens, and the rulers of this earth; instead he was born in a stable, and the good news was first proclaimed to common shepherds on the night shift.

Notice the shepherds' reaction to the appearance of the angel: They feared a great fear! It may be that Luke means to indicate the shepherds' piety with this report, so that "fear" is "fear of the Lord"; but nothing in the text makes this plain. It is more likely that the glory of the angels evoked a sheer passivity on the part of the shepherds who were simply awed by the event. Yet notice, too, that the shepherds are not left in the grips of fear; they are called out of their fright as the angel proclaims the good news, which becomes a sign to which they are to attend. Inherent in the good news of God's grace is a calling to action.

One should not overlook the deep irony at the heart of the angel's declaration. God has given the world a savior, Christ the Lord; and the arrival of this savior is the cause for great joy. But the savior is a baby, born in humble circumstance that both contrast and reveal the true character of God's power and glory. And so, the angels sing—proclaiming God's glory, which results in the true peace of the world.

(C) In the final verses of the reading (15-20) we see that curiosity did not kill the cat of the nighttime shepherds of Bethlehem. No sooner had the angels departed than the shepherds turned to investigate the good news! The telling of God's saving grace produced action in the lives of the shepherds. What they did about the care of the flock is anybody's guess, but clearly they moved swiftly to see the highly acclaimed baby with their own eyes.

For those viewing this text with homiletical eyes, the various actions of the characters are remarkable. On the one hand, Mary experienced the results of the operation of grace and meditated on the events. On the other hand, in the shepherds we see the second evangelists (the angels were the first). Having seen the baby they set about to spread the good news, and their own proclamations now produced wonder among those who heard the story. Moreover, notice that the shepherds are not suddenly made celebrities by having had a visit from the angels and by having seen God's savior. Far from getting swollen heads, the shepherds focused away from themselves, first, by sharing the good news, and second, by worshiping God! Theocentric faith in reaction to christocentric salvation is the substance and shape of Christianity.

CHRISTMAS EVE/CHRISTMAS DAY: THE CELEBRATION

These lessons are based on those traditionally read at the second Mass on Christmas Day, the "Shepherds' Mass," celebrated at dawn, the first Mass having been celebrated at midnight. In general Protestant use, there is no reason why they may not be employed for any of the services of Christmas Eve or Christmas Day.

The song of the angels in the Gospel lesson is the basis for the ancient hymn, the "Gloria in Excelsis Deo" (Glory be to God on high). Traditionally this hymn has been used at the beginning of the Eucharist, but is omitted during Advent so that its use is more remarkable when the Church joins its voice again with the angels in the services of Christmas. Various settings for it may be found in the service music section of any number of recent hymnals. Older hymnals will tend to have only the Old Scottish Chant arrangement. The hymn, "Angels We Have Heard on High," with its chorus of "Gloria in excelsis Deo" may also be used in relation to this Gospel reading. The carol, "While Shepherds Watched Their Flocks by Night," can be used to summarize the Gospel reading. Its last stanza may also be used by itself as a form of the "Gloria in excelsis." "Hark! the Herald Angels Sing," with its rigorous theological language, is also based on this Gospel lesson.

The preacher may wish to note that Luke's Gospel both begins and ends with an announcement of great joy. In Luke 2 the angels announce a "great joy" to the shepherds. Luke 24:52 describes the disciples after the Ascension returning to Jerusalem with "great joy." Joy brackets the events of Christ's earthly ministry. The bulletin cover may employ a form of script to reproduce the closing lines of the medieval "First Shepherds' Play" and so reinforce the theme of joy for this service:

Together in joy,
Our mirth now employ
To the praise of this boy
Sing we for ay.
["The First Shepherds' Play" in *The Wakefield Mystery Plays,* Martial
Rose, ed., (Garden City, N.Y.: Anchor Books, 1961), p. 206]

The epistle lesson reminds us, while we are celebrating the birth of
Jesus, of our own rebirth through baptism and confirmation (water of
rebirth and renewal by the Holy Spirit). This is a healthy emphasis to
make in order to relate the Christmas message to our actual involvement in the Church, the body of Christ. The birth of Jesus is intended to
result in our rebirth; it is not an end in itself. Baptismal thanksgivings
recall how Jesus was "nurtured in the water of a womb," and one of
Cranmer's Christmas collects makes plain the connection between
incarnation and regeneration. It fits well as an opening prayer preparing
the faithful to hear the lessons:

Almighty God, you have given your only-begotten Son to take our
nature upon him, and to be born of a pure virgin: Grant that we, who
have been born again and made your children by adoption and grace,
may daily be renewed by your Holy Spirit; through our Lord Jesus
Christ, to whom with you and the same Spirit be honor and glory, now
and for ever. (*The Book of Common Prayer*, p. 213)

First Sunday After Christmas

Old Testament Texts

Both Isaiah 61:10–62:3 and Psalm 148 incorporate aspects of the hymn of praise. Yet each text goes in a different direction with its exultation. Isaiah 61:10–62:3 turns abruptly at the begining of chapter 62 into a complaint or charge against God, while Psalm 148 uses praise as an occasion to teach fellow worshipers about creation and God's sovereignty.

The Lesson: *Isaiah 61:10–62:3*

Praise or Complaint?

Setting. See the discussion for Christmas, Second Proper in this volume concerning the larger structure of Isaiah 60–62. A brief reading of Isaiah 61:10–62:3 suggests that Isaiah 61:10-11 and 62:1-3 are distinct units. The former unit is a hymn of praise or thanksgiving. It follows the form-critical structure of a call to praise ("I will sing . . . " v. 10*a*) followed by reasons ("because he clothed . . . " v. 10*b*) and it ends by expressing a hope that God will bring salvation to completion (v. 11). Some scholars would even separate v. 11 from v. 10 since it looks to the future rather than presenting a past cause for praise. Isaiah 62:1-3 is clearly a distinct unit from 61:10-11, and it introduces a new set of motifs (the inability of the prophet to keep silent and the renaming of Jerusalem). Furthermore, vv. 1-3 are not themselves an independent unit since the actual renaming of Jerusalem does not occur until v. 4. The form-critical analysis suggests that Isaiah 61:10–62:3 not be interpreted as a single unit, but as two distinct texts.

Structure. The distinction between Isaiah 61:10-11 and 62:1-3 that was evident from a form-critical analysis is reinforced by looking at the larger literary structure. Isaiah 61:10-11 provides a conclusion to the thematic development in Isaiah 61, while 62:1-5 develops many motifs that continue through Isaiah 62. For discussion of 61:10-11 in the larger context of Isaiah 61 see the Third Sunday of Advent, Year B.

Isaiah 61:10-11 presents a fairly tight structure. It consists of a call to praise (v. 10), a reason for praise that includes two analogies (v. 11), a reason for hope that includes two analogies (v. 11a), and a concluding statement of hope (v. 11b). The structure illustrates how the unit moves from the prophet's personal experience of salvation to a larger vision of how God will act in the world.

Isaiah 62:1-3 does not function as a coherent unit and should be extended to v. 5. If we interpret the "I" of v. 1 as the prophet (see Christmas, Second Proper), then the unit separates into three parts. Verses 1-2a are the prophet's charge against God and his decision to speak in place of a silent God. The prophet redirects his speech from God to Zion in vv. 2b-4a in order to describe her name change from "Forsaken" to "My Delight Is in Her." The unit ends in vv. 4b-5 by providing the reason for the change of name.

Significance. The combination of Isaiah 61:10-11 and 62:1-3 into a single text is problematic. The best way to pursue this text for preaching is to make a decision to focus on one of the two parts and disregard the other.

A central theme of Isaiah 61:10-11 is salvation. The theme of salvation is introduced as a present reality in the life of the prophet. Note how the content of salvation is described as the gift of righteousness (v. 10) in which God has clothed the prophet. See Psalm 97 in Christmas, Second Proper for discussion of righteousness as a quality arising from worship. The genre of a praise hymn suggests that worship is also the setting of Isaiah 61:10-11. The prophet turns to the metaphor of marriage clothing to describe the character of righteousness and the relationship it engenders between himself and God. Verse 11 leaves the imagery of salvation within worship and turns our focus outside the cult. Notice how the images shift to creation (the earth and a garden), and how righteousness is no longer a present reality, but a future hope for the prophet. The movement in this text from worship to an idealized world indicates that the passage is eschatological. What this means for preaching is that the personal character of salvation within the context of worship must be emphasized, but that it cannot be the end of our conception of salvation. Rather salvation must move beyond ourselves to a confession about God's transformation of a new creation (a theme also found in the response of Psalm 148). This is indicated in the text when the prophet moves from his personal salvation to a confession of hope that salvation will one day be completed, which is symbolized with the metaphor of righteousness springing forth before all nations.

Isaiah 62:1-5, too, is about salvation, but it begins with a complaint, rather than a thanksgiving hymn. The complaint is that salvation should be much more evident in Jerusalem than it is. Frequently the absence of God's salvation is described with the metaphor of divine silence. Recall, for example, how the lament in Isaiah 63:7–64:12 (First Sunday of Advent, Year B) ended with the prophetic question of whether God would remain silent. The assumption in Isaiah 62:1-5 is that God is all too silent and the prophet cannot bear it. Thus he complains to God and states in vv. 1-2a that for the sake of Zion he will not keep silent even though God may presently be silent. The prophet then turns his attention to Jerusalem in vv. 2b-4a and audaciously speaks a word of salvation in place of God. The core of the prophet's message is that Jerusalem will experience a reversal and that it will be symbolized through a name change. The reason given for the name change in vv. 4b-5 is because of God's changed attitude toward Jerusalem, which will result in a marriage. (This metaphor of marriage is the clearest point of contact between the two lectionary texts.) The logic of the text is not really completed at v. 5 because we do not know why the prophet can act so audaciously by speaking for a silent God. Verses 6-12 provide this information (see Christmas, Second Proper). The reason why the prophet can be so bold as to speak for God is because he has proof of God's promises of salvation, which he not only believes in but on which he is even willing to call God to task. It is for this reason that he places watchmen or sentinels on the wall of Jerusalem who must remind God day and night of his promises.

The Response: *Psalm 148*

A Hymn of Praise

Setting. Psalm 148 is probably best categorized as a hymn of praise in which imperatival forms of the verb predominate (note the repetition of the imperative *Praise!* or *Let them praise!* in vv. 1, 2, 3, 4, 5, 7, 13, 14). The scope of the psalm is so wide in its call to praise that all aspects of creation are included. This larger vision gives rise to a second characteristic of this hymn, which is the strong presence of wisdom motifs, especially evident in the list of the natural order as those called upon to praise God.

Structure. The psalm separates into two parts, vv. 1-6 and 7-14. Verses 1-6 are a call to praise God from heaven, while vv. 7-14 repeat the command but this time from the earth. Each of these sections further separates into three parts: (1) Each section begins with a command to praise (from heaven, vv. 1-4 and from earth, vv. 7-12). (2) The command is followed in each case with a summary statement, which includes a reason why God should be praised (vv. 5 and 13). This section is signaled in each case through the repetition of the phrase, "Let them praise the name of the Lord" (vv. 5*a* and 13*a*). The reason for praise from the hosts of heaven is that God created them (v. 5*b*), while earthly creatures must praise God because only the Lord is exalted on earth (v. 13*b*). (3) Finally, each section ends with a summary statement about God (vv. 6 and 14) in relationship to the hosts of heaven and earth (specifically Israel).

Significance. Psalm 148 is about praise. When read as a response to Isaiah 61:10-11 it emphasizes how God's salvation must extend beyond the cult to include the entire creation. When it is read as a response to Isaiah 62:1-5 the ending in v. 14 stands out, since this concluding confession of confidence provides interpretation for understanding the boldness of the prophet.

New Testament Texts

Both texts for this Sunday focus, in the words of Galatians, on the moment "when the fullness of time had come," when "God sent his Son, born of a woman, born under the law"; and both texts celebrate redemption through adoption, again in the words of Galatians, that God did this "in order to redeem those who were under the law, so that we might receive adoption as children."

The Epistle: *Galatians 4:4-7*

The Inheritance of Salvation

Setting. Paul's letter to the Galatians is one of his so-called "major" writings. The problem he faces is that the believers in the churches in Galatia have come under the influence of a group of outsiders (other early Christian missionaries). The message of the preachers who came to Galatia after Paul had established congregations in that region was different from the basic gospel Paul had preached. These later preachers declare the saving work of God in Christ, and they insist that God's work through Christ means that Gentiles who become Christians are obligated to observe critical portions of Jewish law—specifically, circumcision, certain calendar events, and dietary restrictions. Paul's letter is a complex argument designed to stop the Galatians from becoming law-observant, for he understands that to embrace the law is to deny the complete sufficiency of God's work for salvation in Jesus Christ. Specifically, in Galatians 4:1-7 Paul argues by analogy that the Galatians are adults in Christ, not minors under the law.

Structure. Paul's logic in this analogical argument about the salvation of the Galatians is clear: God is the actor who sent forth his Son (not the law!). The purpose of God's sending was the achievement of salvation for humans. God's work in Jesus Christ means that those who believe the message of God's work in Christ are now children of God. Older homeliticians could have simply fleshed out these points and added a poem—and, indeed, Paul's rhetoric is still suggestive.

Significance. Paul attempts to persuade the Galatians of the sufficiency of God's salvation in Jesus Christ and to dissuade them of the need for the law by arguing on the model of adults versus minors as heirs to an estate. Paul declares that an heir is always an heir, but as a minor an heir has not yet been invested in the inheritance. Instead, minor heirs are under guardians or trustees who are, in fact, over the heirs (despite the heirs' true status) until the appointed time of inheritance arrives.

The argument functions almost as an allegory. The heirs are persons of faith (in relation to Jesus Christ). Yet, before the Christ-event they were minors; and, as such, they were under guardians ("the elemental spirits of the world"—including the law!). For the Gentiles before Christ these elemental spirits were lesser gods, angels, demons, and so on; but, now for Paul's point in argumentation, the focus is the law.

Paul declares that the appointed time of inheritance was the time of Jesus Christ. Thus, the Galatians (and all other believers) are, therefore, fully vested and fully free from the overlordship of former guardians. For believers, the law and other elemental spirits are completely irrelevant!

In the verses of our lesson Paul seems to employ the logic of an early Christian confession or creed (see 4:4 and compare Romans 8:3-4). Notice 4:4 where

—God is the subject
—the verb is "to send"
—the object of the sending is the Son
—the purpose of the sending is the salvation of humanity.

God's act in the Son accomplishes salvation. God's work in Jesus Christ, not human effort in keeping the law, guarantees salvation and sets humans into a right relation to God—an old message that bears repeating since we humans never seem to "get it."

The Gospel: *Luke 2:22-40*

God's Salvation in the Flesh!

Setting. As we noticed in relation to the Gospel lesson for the Fourth Sunday of Advent, Luke's account of the birth of Jesus is told in such a way that incidents related to the annunciation, birth, circumcision, and naming of John the Baptist precede and alternate with the same kinds of events in the life of Jesus. In Luke 1:5-25 the birth of John is foretold, and in Luke 1:26-38 the forthcoming birth of Jesus is announced. Then, Luke 1:57-66 tells of the birth, circumcision, and naming of John; and later, Luke 2:1-21 (especially vv. 1-7, 21) narrates the birth, circumcision, and naming of Jesus. Along the lines of this pattern, the materials in Luke 2:22-40 form an imprecise parallel to the prophetic utterance of Zechariah in Luke 1:63*b*-80.

Structure. Luke offers a triptych in these verses telling of the presentation of the infant Jesus in the Temple. The elements constituting these three scenes reach backward and forward across the expanse of tradition and draw selectively on key portions of the whole in order to compose the scene at hand. Although there are a striking variety of characters and currents in this text, the reader should see that Jesus is the focus of Luke's story despite the complex contents that the verses comprise.

Significance. The first minor panel views Jesus in the context of family in relation to the law (2:22-24). The best of Israel's traditional piety frames, forms, and directs the life of Jesus' family. Luke is at pains in this passage to make clear that Jesus was born and raised in a family that was devoted to observance of the law. Three times in these verses (22, 23, 24) and twice in other portions of the presentation account (vv. 27, 39), Luke mentions the law in such a way that it is clear that the law was the norm for Jesus' family's life.

The central, major panel is concerned with Jesus in the context of Israel's expectations, prophecy, devotion, and proclamation (vv. 25-38). As a concern with the law influenced the composition of the first panel of Luke's triptych, so at the top of this second panel Luke introduces in three rapidly repeated references to the Holy Spirit (vv. 25, 26, 27) another major motif of this presentation scene. Simeon's coming to the Temple at the time that Jesus' family presented him was no mere chance occurrence. Although Simeon's life was permeated with the presence of the Spirit (v. 25) and although he enjoyed the privilege of the insight of inspiration (v. 26), he lived a life that was, nevertheless, Spirit-directed (v. 27). Simeon was possessed by the Spirit, he did not possess the Spirit; therefore, he did not rest on the cushion of grace, rather he walked under the canopy of grace in the path set forth for him.

Luke's telling of the story of the Presentation brings the motifs of law and Spirit together as the Spirit-filled Simeon encounters the law-observant family of Jesus in the Temple. It is both striking and appropriate that law, Spirit, and Temple come together in this narrative to provide a theological context for the words that Simeon will speak over the baby Jesus. As Simeon holds the infant Jesus in his arms, he speaks prophetic words. In vv. 29-32 Luke records the lines of the well-known *Nunc Dimittis*. This oracle has the form of a prayer of petition. Simeon's words acknowledge that in looking upon the baby Jesus he knows, through the inspiration of the Holy Spirit, that he is regarding God's promised salvation. Simeon's recognition is not only that God has brought to fulfillment the promise to Israel but also that his own God-given lot, one day to behold God's salvation, was complete.

As a whole the *Nunc Dimittis* presents a rich combination of the language and thought of the latter portion of Isaiah (see, for example, portions of Isaiah 40; 42; 46; 49; 52; and 66). There are three points of striking continuity between Isaiah's prophetic oracles and Simeon's prophetic utterance in the *Nunc Dimittis:* (1) God is the actor in the bringing of salvation. Salvation is God's work, not the result of human actions. (2) God's salvation is universal in scope, so it includes Gentiles and Jews alike. The promise of salvation came from God to Israel, but the accomplishment of salvation affects all humans regardless of their religious or ethnic background. (3) God's delivery of salvation in Jesus brings glory to Israel, not as the privileged possessors of God's favor, but as God's chosen servant people through whom God has worked to bring forth the salvation achieved in Jesus.

Along with Simeon the prophetess Anna appears in the Temple alongside Jesus' family. She personifies the faith and piety of Israel in the same way that Simeon did. The text does not narrate an encounter between Anna and Joseph, Mary, and Jesus; nor does Luke offer a record of Anna's words. But her reaction to the presentation of Jesus scores two crucial points: (1) Anna gives thanks to God. This is the first and appropriate response of those recognizing the significance of Jesus as the one in whom God accomplishes the promise of salvation. (2) Anna "spoke of [Jesus] to all who were looking for the redemption of Israel." This report emphasizes once more that Jesus is the fulfillment of God's promise of salvation, but of equal or greater importance here is the pattern of Anna's action. The good news is not a private possession to be received and hoarded; rather the good news must be shared, as Anna demonstrated.

In the second minor panel Luke views Jesus in the context of family and life (vv. 39-40). Once again the reader learns of the family of Jesus' dedication to the observance of the law. Having "performed everything according to the law of the Lord" the family returned to Galilee. Luke relocates the family geographically in v. 39, which is a necessary narrative device; but his deeper concerns come through in the statement in v. 40, "The child grew and became strong, filled with wisdom; and the favor of God was upon him." This remark testifies both to the humanity of Jesus and to the divine grace that was upon him as he was "filled with wisdom."

CHRISTMAS 1: THE CELEBRATION

The Gospel lesson for today is the narrative of that event in the life of our Lord which is known as The Presentation of Christ in the Temple. Because it occurred on the fortieth day after the nativity, in conformity with the Levitical law (Leviticus 12:2-4), it is observed as a special day in many churches on February 2. Today, however, provides an opportunity (for those churches that do not observe the calendar that closely) to explore the theological content of this portion of Luke's narrative.

First, this trip to the Temple, as does the circumcision described in the preceding verse, promotes the keeping of the law. Luke goes to great pains to portray Christ as being both subject to and obedient to the law. Luke does not exalt the law for its own sake, as an objective authority; rather he demonstrates that Christ, by being subject to the law, is the only one who can free us from the law. In the act of circumcision (which will be discussed more fully in the next section on the Holy Name of Jesus), Jesus first sheds his blood in subjection to the law. On Calvary his blood will be shed for all humankind to achieve for us what we cannot achieve for ourselves. Again, the Lucan birth narratives derive their meaning from the Passion and the Paschal mystery.

Second, in keeping with Luke's other theme of ministry to the poor and outcast, Mary brings as an offering "two turtledoves or two pigeons," the option allowed to the poor who cannot afford to offer a sheep (Leviticus 12:8). Again, Luke stresses Christ's identification with the poor.

If the decision is made to concentrate on the theme of the Presentation for this service, worship leaders may prefer to use the other lessons that the lectionary assigns to February 2 when it is observed as the Presentation of Christ in the Temple: Malachi 3:1-4, Psalm 84 or 24:7-10, and Hebrews 2:14-18.

If today's epistle as appointed is used, the same opening prayer that was listed above for Christmas Eve/Day would be also appropriate, because it was in fact this epistle for which the prayer was originally composed. An emphasis on the Presentation, however, suggests the use of the following from the Church of England's *Alternative Service Book 1980.*

> Almighty Father,
> whose Son Jesus Christ was presented in the Temple
> and acclaimed the glory of Israel and the light of the nations;
> grant that in him we may be presented to you
> and in the world may reflect his glory;
> through Jesus Christ our Lord.

Today's Gospel lesson also includes the great evening canticle of the Church, the Song of Simeon or *Nunc Dimittis* (Luke 2:29-32). It is also used in the Orthodox liturgy as the concluding hymn. Three versions of it may be found in *The Presbyterian Hymnal* (1990), nos. 603-605.

The following text by Henry Pye, sung to Regent Square, makes either a fine opening hymn for this day or a response to the Gospel lesson.

> In his temple now behold him;
> See the long-expected Lord!
> Ancient prophets had foretold him;
> God has now fulfilled his word.
> Now to praise him, his redeemed

Shall break forth with one accord.
In the arms of her who bore him,
Virgin pure, behold him lie,
While his aged saints adore him,
Ere in perfect faith they die:
Alleluia! Alleluia!
Lo, the incarnate God most high!

Jesus, by your Presentation,
When they blest you, weak and poor,
Make us see your great salvation,
Seal us with your promise sure;
And present us, in your glory,
To your Father, cleansed and pure.

Holy Name of Jesus

Old Testament Texts

Numbers 6:22-27 is the priestly benediction or blessing. Psalm 8 is a hymn that celebrates the creative power of God (as did Psalm 148 last week) while also pondering the status of humans in the world.

The Lesson: *Numbers 6:22-27*

Blessing and Magic

Setting. The larger literary context of the priestly benediction has remained a puzzle for scholars. It occurs without much warning after the laws dealing with Nazirites (Numbers 6:1-21). If we change our focus from its literary context and raise the question of how the priestly benediction functioned in ancient Israel, several important features of the blessing arise. First, not just anyone can bestow blessing. Verse 22 makes it clear that this authority is limited to the Aaronic priesthood. There is some inner-biblical debate on this point, since Deuteronomy 21:5 expands this function to all Levitical priests. But the debate actually underscores the central point that the power to bless is not an egalitarian gift. Having the power to bless creates a real distinction between priest (clergy) and laity. Second, the benediction is meant to function in the context of worship, for it is the realm of worship in which the priest is meant to function. Third, v. 23 underscores how blessing is interpreted to be a communal gift. There is debate over this point with some scholars arguing that blessing could also be bestowed on an individual during a time of sacrifice. However we might answer this debate in all of its details, it is clear that the priestly benediction in Numbers 6:23 is focused primarily on the whole community of Israel. Leviticus 9:22-23 provides an excellent example of the three points listed above, when Aaron is singled out to conclude the first public worship service of Israel by bestowing a blessing on the entire congregation.

Structure. Numbers 6:22-27 separates into three parts: vv. 22-23 provide an introduction to the benediction; vv. 24-26 are the blessing formula; and v. 27 provides concluding commentary concerning how the blessing is transmitted.

The benediction has a simple structure, which consists of three lines, each of which contains central word pairs: bless-keep (protect), shine-grace, lift-peace. The name Yahweh (the Lord) occurs once in each line in association with the first verb.

Yahweh bless you	and keep you
Yahweh make his face to shine upon you	and be gracious to you
Yahweh lift up his countenance upon you	and give you peace

The structure raises the question of whether the six words describe distinct actions of God, or whether they are meant to be interpreted in groups of two, with the first word in each line describing an activity of God upon the worshiper, and the second verb describing the results of God's actions. The single occurrence of the divine name favors a reading that clusters the verbs in groups of two as we have done.

Significance. The central task in preaching this text is to explore what blessing means. Is the bestowing of a blessing something that is sacramental or is it no more than a socially polite activity? What is it that we receive at the close of a worship service when the minister bestows God's blessing on us? Is there real divine power being transmitted here or is she or he simply telling us that the service is nearly over? This latter point is probably closer to the function of blessing in contemporary worship, and this creates a problem for interpreting and for using the priestly benediction.

The best way to enter into an interpretation of Numbers 6:22-27 is to begin at the other point in the spectrum with the observation that blessing is a magical power. Such a starting point is consistent with the culture of ancient Israel. For an illustration of the magical power of blessing read the story of Isaac and Esau in Genesis 27:30-38, where Jacob literally steals the blessing by coaxing it out of Isaac's mouth, and, even though Esau tells his father as much, Isaac responds that he can't undo it. Once the blessing has been given, it has a power of its own. It is as though the rabbit cannot be put back into the hat, and the result of this is that Jacob runs off with the blessing. Such a view of blessing as magic is powerful because it makes the salvation of God very concrete and very real. Yet it is also dangerous because the con-creteness of a magical blessing, with a power of its own, makes the salvation of God extremely vulnerable to manipulation. And, indeed, the story of Jacob, Esau, and Isaac illustrates this very point. Because of this two-sidedness to the magical power of blessing, there is a ten-sion in biblical texts concerning the divine power to bless. The tension is evident in the tendency throughout the Old Testament to play down the magical aspect of blessing, even though it never completely leaves this realm.

The priestly benediction provides illustrations of the tension sur-rounding blessing. Blessing is not an otherworldly idea in vv. 24-26. Rather it includes very concrete things like protection from misfortune, and all the good gifts that result in a life of wholeness or peace. Such a bestowing of divine blessing is not the equivalent of sending someone a greeting card. If anything, the writers of the text are all too aware of the magical power of blessing, and they try to avoid the dangers that accom-pany such a strong belief with the introduction and the conclusion to the benediction. Notice how the introduction in vv. 22-23 underscores that only a special class of holy people (the priests) can handle the blessing. Blessing is not a casual activity. Furthermore, the conclusion under-scores just how close to the world of magic the text actually is, since the author must make it clear that the priest does not possess the blessing independently of God. Rather the priest has the power to place God's name on Israel (to target them?) with the result that God then blesses the people. The implication of the text is that worship is the target location for receiving God's blessing, and that it is a real and independent power that can be let loose in the congregation.

The text is a problem for preachers because we tend to view the movement away from magic in the Old Testament as an affirmation of our own secular worldview, where the thought of blessing as something sacramental is dismissed at the outset. Such a conclusion would be unfortunate, because our problem is just the reverse of ancient Israel—namely, that our secular worldview isn't sacramental enough.

The Response: *Psalm 8*

What Are Humans?

Setting. Psalm 8 is a hymn of praise, which modulates between an individual voice (vv. 1*b*-8) and a community refrain (vv. 1*b*, 9). The central motif of the community refrain is the celebration of the name of God, which accounts for the inclusion of this psalm on this Sunday.

Structure. Psalm 8 separates into two sections: vv. 1-4 and 5-9. The community refrain begins the first section (v. 1*b*) and concludes the last section (v. 9), with the result that the praise of God's name throughout the earth frames the entire psalm. The voice of the individual singer takes up the middle portion of the psalm. Within this section, the central theme of the psalm appears to be the question of v. 4: "What are human beings that you are mindful of them?" Most commentators agree that this question and the description of the role of humans in creation that follows in vv. 6-8 is based on the account of creation of humans in Genesis 1:26. Thus Psalm 8 should be read as inner-biblical reflection on Genesis 1.

Significance. Psalm 8 is somewhat unusual in that it is a hymn of praise that addresses God in the second person ("you"). The use of the second person establishes a certain intimacy in the relationship between singer and God, which is striking because it contrasts with the vast (and impersonal) creation imagery that is the subject matter of much of the hymn (God is sovereign, majestic, creator of heavens, moon and stars, etc.). This contrast between the intimate relationship of singer and God, on the one hand, and the vastness of the creation order, on the other, is an important point of entry into interpreting Psalm 8, for it provides the background for the central question in v. 4. What are humans to God in the larger context of the universe? On such a large stage our first response would be that humans are insignificant to the larger drama of creation. Psalm 8 is a hymn of praise because just the opposite is true. God is not only mindful of earthbound mortals (v. 4), but he has even given them a formative role as actors on the large stage of creation. One suspects that this paradox (between the insignificance of humans in the larger order of creation and the degree of attention that God bestows on them) may provide insight for interpreting v. 2, which has no parallel any place in Scripture. Perhaps it is the frail human mortals who are the babes of v. 2

that God has chosen as a defense against evil, even though God had so many more resources at his disposal ("You have set your glory above the heavens."). This fact is then what prompts the wonder and awe of the psalmist concerning the position of humans in the larger drama of God's creation.

New Testament Texts

The humility and humanity of Jesus Christ are themes inherent in the lessons for this Sunday. Yet the text from Philippians is a poetic meditation on the person of Christ, while the passage from Luke narrates the events following the poetic doxology and declaration of the angels to the shepherds of Bethlehem.

The Epistle: *Philippians 2:5-13*

Celebrating Christ Through Devotion

Setting. The Philippian congregation was the first European church founded by Paul, and it was one with which he maintained a very positive relationship. He was in prison at the time he penned this letter, and he seems to have written for several reasons: (1) to thank the Philippians for their support, physical and spiritual; (2) to discuss Epaphroditus' visit to him in behalf of the Philippians; and (3) to address difficulties and potential problems in the life of the church. Paul spends time early in the body of the letter exhorting the Philippians to unity, beginning at 1:27. In the course of that admonition he holds Christ himself up in a formal fashion as the model and source of Christian harmony.

Structure. Since the late 1920s scores of scholars have studied Philippians 2:(5)6-11, attempting both to demonstrate that this portion of Philippians is a "Christ-hymn" from the life of the early church and to determine the hymn's structure, origin, authorship, and theology. At the heart of debate about structure is whether the "hymn" is concerned with celebrating two movements (Christ's humble emptying into human form and Christ's exaltation to heavenly Lordship) or three states (pre-existence/human life/resurrection-exaltation). While these issues are still studied and debated, interpreters are moving toward a middle ground that recognizes the importance of all the elements of both schemes. Whatever the analysis, however, v. 5 is regarded as prose, leading up to the hymn; and vv. 6-11 are seen as the "hymn" per se. Verses 12-13 apply the teaching of the hymn about Christlikeness to the lives of the Philippians.

Significance. It is crucial to recognize the range and force of the theological and christological statements contained in the Christ-hymn. Five major thoughts are articulated.

First, the remarks about Jesus Christ's being in the form of God is a metaphorical expression of the conviction of his pre-existence. With notable exceptions, few interpreters read the line otherwise. The importance of this interpretation should not be missed. Here, in one of the earliest preserved documents of Christianity is the confession of Christ's pre-existence. Often historians assume that belief in pre-existence came later in the development of Christian doctrine, but Philippians is testimony to the contrary. Equally remarkable is that Paul, the former Jew, includes and approves such a belief, for there is no evidence that Paul had abandoned Jewish monotheism to make this statement.

Second, Christ's earthly existence is declared using the metaphor of slavery. What does it mean to say that Christ took the form of a slave? The metaphor points to his humble obedience to the will of God and to his faithful service to his fellow human beings as he did God's will.

Third, we hear of Christ's death. The mention of the cross in connection with the death points to the degree of humiliation Christ suffered in order to be faithful to God and humankind. His service was costly. He did not live to a ripe old age and enjoy the fruits of his happy life of service. Indirectly Paul is telling the Philippians (and us) that the Lord died in order to be obedient and faithful. Thus, what can disciples expect?

Fourth, Christ's exaltation-resurrection is declared. The phrase, "wherefore also God," introduces this element of the confession. Clearly Christ's being raised and his subsequent exalted status are God's work. Notice, too, that the language ("wherefore") reaches back and relates God's action to Christ's own emptying and self-sacrifice.

Fifth, we learn of Christ's cosmic rule. His self-giving unto death, which issued in God's exalting him, makes him the ruler of the cosmos. The phrases describing the "knees" indicate that all the denizens of heaven, earth, and hell will acknowledge Christ's rule. And the point of that rule is given with the words, "unto the glory of God the Father."

Finally vv. 12-13 exhort the Philippians to live in the manner in which Christ lived and, now, to which Paul is calling them. These verses are a well-known and often-quoted statement—at least in part.

Almost anyone raised in the Church can cite, "work out your own salvation with fear and trembling"; but few indeed can finish the sentence, "for God is the one working in/among you, both to will and to work for his good pleasure." The translation of this text in the NRSV ("for it is God who is at work in you, enabling you both to will and to work for his good pleasure") is inaccurate and misleading, representing an attempt to mitigate Paul's startling statement that God tinkers with the precious human will! Paul's God is not merely a wimpish enabler, he is the Lord of creation who works on and with the human will in order to accomplish his purposes. This does not mean that humans are puppets on a string, but it does mean that we are not hermetically sealed holders of a totally free will. We are able to work out our own salvation precisely because God is at work in us, and that's the gospel! God cares so much that we are not merely left to our own devices.

The Gospel: *Luke 2:15-21*

To Hear and to Hold God's Word

Setting. Luke 2:1-21 is actually one large story sequence concerned with the events around the birth of Jesus. There are three distinct subsections of the narrative: 2:1-7 sets the birth in context (Rome, Palestine, Bethlehem, manger); 2:8-14 tells of the angels' annunciation of the birth of Jesus to the shepherds; and 2:15-20 records the reaction(s) of the shepherds to the message of the angels. Verse 21 brings the sequence to a conclusion by briefly reporting the circumcision and naming of Jesus.

Structure. The story is a complex cluster of ideas and activities. We are given a series of reactions by groups and individuals to the birth of Jesus: The going, seeing, announcing, and worshipful activity of the shepherds; the hearing and the wonder of those who heard the shepherds; and Mary's remembering and pondering of the events. The short account of circumcision and naming tell, in turn, of actions done specifically in relation to Jesus himself.

Significance. The celebration this Sunday of the Holy Name of Jesus is the reason for the use of this text. Let us begin with v. 21, because it concludes the larger narrative unit in such a way that we may read the previous series of reactions through the lens established in this verse. Notice that in contrast to the earlier scene of the naming of John the Baptist (1:59-66[79]) the story here is concisely told, and the parents of the child are not mentioned. Thus the focus is sharply set on the acts of circumcision and naming, though the story merely mentions circumcision and finds its true focus in the naming of Jesus, an act that fulfills the command of the angel in 1:31. The naming of Jesus is an example of faithful obedience to God's word. Above all, it is in relation to the person of Jesus per se that we find God's word fulfilled. The strong emphasis on Jesus himself is clear in the narration ("when he was circumcised, his name was called Jesus . . . before he was conceived"); here, time is marked in relation to the one named Jesus.

Now, we may consider the various human reactions to the birth of Jesus; we shall do so on the principle of from lesser to greatest. First, the larger population—namely, "all who heard it"—are astonished by the report of the shepherds. Yet, there is nothing in the narrative to suggest that the astonishment is anything other than an end in itself. Luke gives us no hint that these people moved even to investigate that of which they heard. Second, the shepherds represent a slightly more active response to the good news. They heard, they went, they saw, and they even made known to those in Bethlehem what was made known to them. But Luke tells us only that they returned to their flocks praising and glorifying God for God's great accomplishment(s); we do not hear that after their return to the flocks, the shepherds made the news known further. The praise by the shepherds echoes the angels' praise, and their proclamation of Jesus' birth anticipates later early Christian proclamation of the good news of Jesus Christ, but for now they fall silent after having responded to God's initiative. Third, Mary is the only adult in the story of the birth of Jesus who reappears in the account of his later ministry. Luke tells us that Mary, and Mary alone, "kept with devotion all these occurrences, interpreting them in her heart." Thus she is enriched, molded, even transformed by the events and the reactions, so that she becomes one who hears the word of God and keeps it— namely, an example of true discipleship (see 11:28).

For Christians seeking inspiration and direction from the Gospel account, we should see that God's work in Jesus elicits a variety of responses. While all those mentioned in this story are presented in a positive light, as we read and ponder the lines of our text, we should see that amazement, curiosity, investigation, proclamation, and worship are attendant actions to the one necessary action of holding God's word in our hearts so that we are refashioned by that word alive in our lives.

HOLY NAME (JAN. 1): THE CELEBRATION

The Revised Common Lectionary provides two sets of propers for January 1: one observes the day as the Festival of the Holy Name, and the other as "New Year's Day." Protestants may be a bit startled by that Festival of the Holy Name, supposing a "Catholic" designation. They may be even more startled to learn that since Vatican II there has been no such festival observed in the Roman Catholic Church (although there is still a votive Mass of the Holy Name). The lectionary is following an ancient tradition in observing January 1 as the Festival of the Holy Name by recognizing that the Lucan chronology places the circumcision and the naming of Jesus on the eighth day after his birth. This is an even older practice than observing January 1 as the beginning of the civil year, which is a comparatively recent practice as historians think of such things. In England, March 25 was considered the beginning of the new year until 1752. This year we will discuss the Holy Name lessons; the lessons for the New Year's Day observance will be found in the Year C series.

In those years when January 1 falls on a Sunday these lessons may take the place of those regularly appointed for the First Sunday After Christmas. The emphasis for the preacher is quite clearly "What's in a name?" Jesus' name is given to him before his birth and it is intended to describe his mission of saving his people from their sins. It is related to an older Hebrew form which means "God is salvation." The preacher may wish to explore the power of names in our culture and how they affect our perceptions, and blessings. What is wrong with "Benedict Arnold" as a series of sounds used to designate a particular individual? Or Jezebel? Why is it that "there is something about that name"? The Old Testament lesson authorizes a priesthood to bless through the power of the Name of God. The liturgical implications here for those who, in the interests of inclusivity, revise nominal formulas to functional or descriptive ones, are worth discussing in the congregation's worship committee or among the ecumenical pastors' lectionary study group. The epistle lesson illustrates how a name reflects the power of its holder. The Gospel lesson deals with both the circumcision and the naming of Jesus. Often in the Church's history we recall a tendency to emphasize the circumcision at the expense of the naming. Until the recent liturgical revisions, the latest centuries have usually referred to January 1 as the Feast of the Circumcision. There are certainly theological affirmations to be made on the basis of the circumcision: Jesus being subject to the law and shedding his blood as a sign of his sacrificial life are two of the most notable. But these are secondary to the giving of the name, for they are illustrative of what the name of Jesus means—God saves. This is the core of that Christmas event we have all been celebrating for a week now.

Protestant devotion to the Holy Name is evident from the widespread use of such hymns and gospel songs as "Take the Name of Jesus with You," "How Sweet the Name of Jesus Sounds," "Jesus! the Name High Over All," "All Hail the Power of Jesus' Name," "O, How I Love Jesus," and "There's Something About That Name." Today's service could make good use of selected stanzas of these hymns as introits and various kinds of liturgical responses. The following collect from the American *Book of Common Prayer* draws together themes from today's lessons:

> Eternal Father, you gave to your incarnate Son the holy
> name of Jesus to be the sign of our salvation: Plant in
> every heart, we pray, the love of him who is the Savior
> of the world, our Lord Jesus Christ; who lives and reigns
> with you and the Holy Spirit, one God, in glory everlasting.

Various monograms or symbols of the Holy Name such as the Chi-Rho, the IHS, and the Ichthus might be used as visuals in today's service. If they have been used earlier to decorate the chrismon tree, attention could be called to them at this time as their meanings are explained. The "Glossary of Christian Symbols" in *The New Handbook of the Christian Year* can be helpful here.

Epiphany of the Lord

Old Testament Texts

Isaiah 60:1-6 is a summons for Zion to see the salvation of God, while Psalm 72:1-7, 10-14 is a prayer for the well-being of the messianic king.

The Lesson: *Isaiah 60:1-6*

Reflected Light

Setting. Isaiah 60:1-6 is perhaps best classified as a theophany—a text that describes the appearance of God. The classical form of theophany in ancient Israel includes a description of the approach of God (God comes or descends) and the reaction of nature (nature fears or trembles), while the context for such appearances of God was often war. An example of a classical account of theophany would be Judges 5:4 where God is described by Deborah as "going out" from Edom to fight Sisera, which prompts the earth "to tremble." Note in Isaiah 60:1-6 the degree to which the prophet has departed from the classical description of theophany. The only natural phenomena in this description of the appearance of God is light, while motifs of war are lacking altogether.

Structure. Isaiah 60:1-6 is not a separate unit of literature. Most scholars agree that all of Isaiah 60 is a literary unity. Yet there are divisions within the chapter that can be followed. The closest smaller division to the lectionary text is Isaiah 60:1-9, which separates into two parts. Verses 1-3 describe the theophany of God to Zion. Verses 4-9 describe the results of theophany with the imagery of the nations flocking to Zion from the land (vv. 4-7) and from the sea (vv. 8-9).

Significance. The central image of the text is light and its function within the text should provide the guidelines for preaching. Several aspects of the light become more apparent by looking at the development of the opening three verses. Three things are noteworthy about v. 1:

First, the presence of God's salvation is imaged as light; second, the light is not a static image, but is used to signify the movement of God toward Zion; and, third, Zion must be summoned to arise (literally, to pull herself up) even though theophany is already taking place ("the glory of the LORD has risen upon you"). The imagery of this last point is far removed from the involuntary reaction of nature to the approach of God. Verse 2 describes two results of theophany: First, light necessarily creates contrast by highlighting darkness in all the places where it is absent; and second, Zion becomes a reflector of divine light. Verse 3 describes the result of theophany in the larger context of the world: The nations will spontaneously travel to the light.

The imagery of light in the opening verses invites comparison to astronomy. If God's salvation is self-generating light, then it would resemble the sun. Zion, on the other hand, is like the moon because it radiates no light. Even though it lacks the ability to generate light, it is able to reflect the light of the sun in a spectacular way, but only when it is positioned correctly in the sky. Thus movement and proper positioning is important for the moon to be visible at all. The call of the prophet for Zion to rise up because its light has come is not a call to generate light, but a call to reflect the light that is present, much like the moon. The challenge of the prophet is that if Zion answers the summons to arise, it will reflect light and thus become a point of focus toward which others will travel. The second part of the text, vv. 4-9, describes the traveler that will journey to Zion if Zion responds to the prophet's call.

The Response: *Psalm 72:1-7, 10-14*

Praying for Messianic Rule

Setting. Psalm 72 can be classified as a royal psalm. A royal psalm was composed for the king in pre-exilic Israel and was probably used in cultic ceremonies in which the king functioned. Psalm 72 focuses primarily on intercession for the king, and the rare subtitle added during the canonical process suggests that Solomon was imagined as an ideal messianic king.

Structure. Psalm 72 is difficult to outline. For purposes of interpretation, the fourteen verses of the lectionary reading might be separated into three sections: vv. 1-7 are an intercessory prayer for the king to rule over Israel; vv. 8-11 extend the intercessory prayer to a request that the king have universal rule; vv. 12-14 provide reasons why the king should rule.

Significance. Two things are noteworthy for interpreting Psalm 72. The first provides a point of continuity with Isaiah 61:1-16, while the second provides a point of contrast.

First, Psalm 72 reflects the point of view of Israel's royal theologians who believed that the king was God's special representative on earth. The opening intercession for the king in vv. 1-2 illustrates this theology, for the psalmist actually requests that God transfer his attributes of righteousness and justice to the king, so that the king could then mediate these qualities to the people. Verses 3-7 describe the effects that the kings mediation of God's attributes could have on the quality of life of the people (land would be prosperous, needy persons would be cared for, oppressors would be crushed, and peace would abound until the moon was extinguished). This role of the king as a mediator of God's attributes is very similar to the role of Zion in Isaiah 60:1-6, since, in Psalm 72 the king, too, is viewed as a reflector of divine righteousness and justice in much the same way that Zion reflected God's light for the prophet.

Second, Psalm 72 contrasts to Isaiah 60:1-6 in describing how the theophany of God is to be universalized, when vv. 8-9 are also included in the reading along with vv. 10-11. Psalm 72:8-11 focuses on the relationship of the king to the other nations by requesting that God provide the king with the power to conquer. Thus the central images are of victory in war (dominion, conquest of foes, tribute, etc.). The setting of war is absent in Isaiah 60:1-6, and thus the dynamic of the relationship between Zion and the nations changes. In Isaiah 60:1-6, Zion becomes a reflector of God's light to the nations rather than a conquering force, which prompts them to journey to it with tribute.

New Testament Texts

The reference to "the eternal purpose" of God "carried out in Christ Jesus our Lord" and, thus, "revealed" and "made known to humankind" makes the epistle lesson particularly appropriate for the celebration of the Epiphany. In turn, the feast of the Epiphany celebrates Matthew's story of the magi from the East to whom appeared a star at the birth of the Christ (the King of the Jews) in Bethlehem—a dramatic account of certain circumstances surrounding Christ's appearance or manifestation.

The Epistle: *Ephesians 3:1-12*

Consider What God Has Done

Setting. Ephesians is a striking document. It seems unrelated to any specific situation but related to every divine and human moment. The epistle falls into two broad parts: Chapters 1–3 are an elaborate, profoundly theological statement, almost esoteric in nature they are so lofty, complex, and even elegant; chapters 4–6 are still elevated in style, expression, and outlook, but here we find statements about the ordering of the everyday life of believers. The theme of this epistle, in both its theological and practical parts, is cosmic reconciliation. Having reminded the readers in chapter 2 of their shameful pasts, of God's merciful provision in Christ, and of the peaceful privilege of being one in Christ despite past differences, Ephesians moves in the opening verses of chapter 3 (this week's lesson) to recall Paul's part in God's work, his understanding of God's purposes, and his and the church's divinely-appointed place(s) in God's intentions.

Structure. The form of this rich statement is that of testimony. Perhaps that tone and purpose should inform the sermon. Dedication to Christ, commission to mission, knowledge of God's "mystery" through revelation, the incorporation of Gentiles into the community of faith, commitment to service because of the grace of divine calling, humility, devotion, providence, and the character of believers' relationship to God through Christ are the nine major themes of the passage. Any one or a combination of these themes can provide the basis for proclamation; indeed, a formidable series of sermons could come from this one text. In the following discussion we shall reflect upon the entire passage in terms of the operation of grace, which unites these manifold themes to one another.

Significance. The mystery of God hidden through previous ages and now revealed plainly is nothing other than the outpouring of God's grace in and through Jesus Christ. The issue of God's grace has achieved a new human situation, bringing into the community of faith those who were once outside its parameters. A previously factionalized and hostile humanity has now, by God's grace, been reconciled to God and simultaneously to itself!

Our lesson from Ephesians declares, celebrates, and meditates on the grandeur of God's grace. God has been astonishingly generous to unworthy humankind. Grace has transformed all relationships, vertical and horizontal. And, as humans have been reconciled to God and to one another, they have been incorporated into a transformed existence that claims their lives as agents of God's grace. Paul is only one example of transformed humanity. Grasped by grace he enjoys the privileges of reconciliation, actively not passively. Paul's experience of grace is at once a personal liberation and a commission to service toward others.

We learn from this text that reconciliation by grace through Jesus Christ was God's eternal purpose. Reconciliation is not merely a desperate divine response to the fractured condition of humanity and creation; rather, this was God's plan all along, because God has ever been a God of grace whose purposes are peace, harmony, and wholeness. The plan is not new, for it is based on the consistency and dependability of God's own person. While grace is not new, it has, from the perspective of Ephesians, been recently revealed in Jesus Christ. We humans know God's grace, we experience God's transforming power, and we clearly discern God's character as we behold Jesus Christ, the manifestation, the appearance, the "Epiphany" of God's grace. Moreover, as the experience of grace is active, directing us into service, it also actively establishes a new, direct, and vital relationship between God and ourselves, so that we approach God in boldness and confidence; these qualities characterize our own new God-given existence.

The Gospel: *Matthew 2:1-12*

The Epiphany of the True King of the Jews

Setting. Chapter 2 of Matthew's Gospel has a certain coherence, but careful reading shows that the material falls into two parts. Matthew 2:1-12 is focused in Bethlehem and is concerned with God's hampering of Herod through the magi, while 2:13-23 shifts the focus from Bethlehem to Egypt and is concerned with God's thwarting of Herod through the actions of Joseph. The stories are related but they may be viewed in isolation from one another as adherence to the lectionary demands.

Structure. Two scenes compose this passage. First, vv. 1-6 tell of the coming of the wise men from the East to Jerusalem. From there they are directed to Bethlehem through quotation of blended texts from Micah 5:1 and II Samuel 5:2. Second, in Bethlehem the magi pay homage to the Christ child before being directed away from Herod and back to their own country. The actions of worship and the gifts seem to allude to Psalm 72:1, 10-11; and Isaiah 60:6. The series of actions by the magi—seeing, seeking, finding, and expressing respect—are all ultimately faithful, joyous acts of worshipful obedience to God's initiative and direction.

Significance. This story is a rich complex of themes that could inspire a series of sermons or a multifaceted single sermon. At the core of the narrative is the idea that God's promises to Israel, of an heir to the throne of David—and, perhaps, even of the appearance of a prophet like Moses—are fulfilled in the birth of Jesus Christ. This theme is particularly prominent because of both Matthew's allusions to Old Testament texts and his outright quotation(s) of Old Testament passages. But beyond the overt employment of scripture, the story in Matthew 2:1-12 conjures memories of God's work with Israel and promises to that nation. The star which brings the magi from the East is reminiscent of the promised star from Jacob (see Numbers 24:17), which became practically a title for the one God would send to deliver Israel. Even the setting in Bethlehem calls up Davidic associations, so that "the Christ" who is born is clearly the fulfillment of God's promise of an heir to David to rule Israel. Herod's hostility (and the subsequent flight to Egypt and return to Nazareth) recalls the hostility of Pharaoh (and the story of Israel's sojourn and Exodus from Egypt).

The appearance of the magi in this story about Jesus' birth shows us the early, positive reaction of Gentiles to God's work in Jesus Christ. The magi are curious, inquisitive, tenacious, reverent, and obedient. They are, however, more than the first Boy Scouts! They are precursors of the later Gentiles who will gladly receive the gospel, responding with appropriate devotion and compliance to God's work and will. They are a prominent outcome of God's work in Christ, incorporating the once excluded Gentiles into the community of faith.

Furthermore, inherent in this story is a striking contrast—between Herod the Great, designated King of the Jews by the Romans, and Jesus Christ, first called King of the Jews here by the magi, later by Pontius Pilate during his Passion, and ultimately by believers who recognize his lordship over life. One king, Herod, seems to perceive God's will; after all he asks about the birthplace of "the Christ"; but in his knowledge he acts strongly to oppose God's work through the anointed one. The other king, Jesus, is born in fulfillment of God's promises, and he will live and die in full devotion and obedience to God's will.

Finally, the story makes profound commentary on the reality of divine revelation. At the outset of the account, we learn of the cosmic dimension of God's revelation in Jesus Christ: A star declares the birth of the child and signifies to those with eyes to see that God's power is being manifested among humans in a most dramatic way. This cosmic act of revelation produces a separation among humans, for some see God's hand in the occurrence and others simply do not. For those who see, the star of revelation is a calling to encounter the person of Jesus Christ. Perhaps the magi acted deliberately to do little more than gratify their natural curiosity over the star, but the result of their response to God's revelation was their worshiping the Christ child. Herod, who did not see, but who after the fact knows that God is at work, reacts in hostility; but his all too inappropriate response is ultimately thwarted by God's redirecting the magi away from the belligerent Herod, who seems only concerned with preserving his position as king of the Jews.

As the magi moved obediently in response to God's cosmic revelation they become personally involved in God's fulfillment of divine promises. Thus they receive even further revelation—this time of the most direct and personal kind. They are not merely called, now they are directed to return to "their own country by another road." The homiletical imagination should not miss the symbolism of "rerouting" that comes from the intervention of divine revelation in the context of human life. The consistent biblical word about revelation is that in its genuine form, revelation always calls us and produces changes in our lives.

THE EPIPHANY: THE CELEBRATION

The Feast of the Epiphany has traditionally been celebrated in the West on January 6, bringing to an end the "twelve days of Christmas" on January 5, or Twelfth Night. Current practice tends to see the Epiphany more as a part of the Christmas celebration rather than the beginning of a new season in its own right. The propers for the time after Epiphany are designed to serve as a meditation on the meaning of that light which shone forth at Christmas for shepherds and for wise men. In that sense the time after Epiphany is an extension of the Christmas proclamation as it deals with various epiphanies. The visit of the wise men is but the first of several "manifestations," which the Gospel lessons will deal with in the coming Sundays, beginning with the baptism of Jesus on the First Sunday After Epiphany and ending with the Transfiguration on the Last Sunday After Epiphany.

Churches that desire to observe the feast of the Epiphany on a Sunday rather than a weekday may elect to do so on the Sunday before January 6, since the following Sunday should always be observed as the Baptism of the Lord. The baptism is an older observance in the church's history, and it is of such importance as to be recognized by all four Gospels.

There is such a wealth of liturgical material relating to this day that liturgical planners will have more difficulty deciding what not to use than otherwise. Two hymns should be mentioned, however, because they are not well known and are disappearing from some collections. This is unfortunate, and it is to be hoped that pastors and music directors will make an effort to reclaim them. One is "Earth Has Many a Noble City," which can be found in the *Episcopal Hymnal 1982* (no. 127). It serves a valuable teaching function by its description of the meaning of the three gifts. Text and tune are in the public domain. The other is "Brightest and Best of the Stars ["Sons" in older editions] of the Morning." Also in the public domain, it can be found in the Episcopal hymnal at no. 117, in the *Lutheran Book of Worship* at no. 84, and in the *Presbyterian Hymnal* at no. 67.

The third stanza of "As with Gladness Men of Old" (tune: Dix) fits well on this day as the offertory response:

> As they offered gifts most rare
> At that manger rude and bare,
> So may we with holy joy,
> Pure, and free from sin's alloy,
> All our costliest treasures bring,
> Christ, to thee, our heavenly King.

Martin Luther allegorized the three gifts in the following way:

Incense is a live confession, full of faith, by which we offer all that we have and are to God. The Wise Men traversed a long distance to bring this gift. Spiritually we can bring it swiftly and easily. The gift of gold is that we should confess Christ as King, laying aside our own esteem and the dictates of our reason and good intentions, that we should present ourselves as foolish, naked, and ready to be ruled. The sons of obedience are tractable, gladly accept their King, and bring all into submission to Christ. The incorrigibles who resist their King fall into tumult, anger, dissension, murmuring, and blasphemy. Thus we see that incense is faith and gold is hope, because faith believes that all things are and ought to be of God, and hope accepts and sustains what faith believes. The myrrh is love. Faith takes us from ourselves, that we should refer everything to God with praise and gratitude. Hope fills us with the concerns of others, that we may endure all in patience without resentment. Love reduces us to that nothing which we were in the beginning, so that we desire neither goods nor anything outside of God, but simply that we should commit ourselves truly to his good pleasure. This is the way of the cross by which we come most speedily to life. (Roland H. Bainton, *The Martin Luther Christmas Book* [Philadelphia: Muhlenberg Press, 1948], pp. 64-65)

Baptism of the Lord (First Sunday After Epiphany)

Old Testament Texts

Genesis 1:1-5 describes the primeval state of watery chaos, while Psalm 29 celebrates the power of God to control the chaotic waters.

The Lesson: *Genesis 1:1-5*

Watery Chaos

Setting. Genesis 1 is a creation mythology. Creation mythologies are common throughout the ancient Near East. The words *creation* and *mythology* require a brief definition to provide background for interpreting Genesis 1:1-5. Genesis 1 is also the Old Testament lesson for Trinity Sunday, Year A.

First, the term *mythology* in the ancient Near Eastern context means something that is often ultimately true. From this starting point we could say that the story of Jesus is mythological because the account of his life goes beyond a three year sequence of historical events and actually becomes a description of the very foundations of our lives in this world. In other words the story of Jesus provides a paradigm that is true throughout time. This meaning runs against our current usage, where myth frequently means the opposite—namely, that a claim is "false" as in the statement, "That's a myth!" which we use when someone lies or when a statement is not factual. This reversal in meaning is partly caused by the elevation of the scientific method in our culture. When we claim that a myth is true, we do not then enter into a dispute about whether we can see, taste, touch, smell, or hear that truth claim. If we do engage in such arguments, our partners in dialogue are likely to assert that our truth claims are "merely" a groundless myth—that is, for the scientist, not subject to positive verification or proof.

Second, the term *creation* signifies the structure of the entire cosmos. Hence creation might be better termed as cosmology in biblical literature. Creation is the preferred genre in the ancient Near East for addressing the ultimate questions about the world, which are the subject matter of mythology. Creation mythologies, therefore, are profoundly theological for they always address at least the following four questions: (1) Who is God? (2) What is the nature or character of this world? (3) What is the relationship between God and this world? And (4) Who are we? or What does it mean to be human in the larger context of God's relationship to this world? Genesis 1:1-5 focuses primarily on the first three questions.

Structure. There is much debate concerning the structure of Genesis 1:1-5, with the primary problems arising in vv. 1-3. The central problem concerns the opening words, "In the beginning. . . . " The Hebrew syntax suggests that this is a temporal clause, which would then be translated like the NRSV ("In the beginning when God created . . . "). Yet the form of the verb, "[God] created" is not what we could expect in a temporal clause, and this creates ambiguity in the opening verse of the Bible. A comparison of the NRSV to the RSV illustrates the ambiguity, since the latter translation plays down the temporal clause ("In the beginning God created . . . "). The reason why this ambiguity has received so much attention is that when the temporal clause is emphasized (as in the NRSV translation), Genesis 1 does not allow for an interpretation of God creating the world from nothing (*creatio ex nihilo*). Such a conclusion has been fearful to people because it appears to weaken the creative power of God. It is doubtful that our writer would have shared such a fear. In any case, our assumptions about what God should or should not do as creator must be set aside, so that the larger issues associated with the structure of Genesis 1:1-3 can be described.

The present interpretation is following the NRSV. Thus Genesis 1:1 is being read as a temporal clause introducing the subject matter of God's project of creation. What makes this decision important for interpretation is that v. 2 is a description of the "stuff" or "uncreated" matter out of which God is going to fashion a world. Verse 2, therefore, is part of the sentence that is begun in v. 1, and it describes chaos before God works on it. Verse 3 is a new sentence, which describes the first act of creation. This action continues through v. 5.

The preceding syntactical analysis allows Genesis 1:1-5 to be outlined into two sections.

I. A Description of Chaos at the Time of Creation (vv. 1-2)
II. A Description of the First Act of Creation (vv. 3-5)

Significance. The central focus for interpreting Genesis 1:1-5 in the larger context of the baptism of Jesus must be v. 2. This verse separates into three clauses, which appear to be a description of chaos: (1) the earth was a formless void, (2) darkness covered the face of the deep, (3) a wind from God swept over the face of the waters. The words used in these three clauses create a whole new set of problems for interpreters. (1) *Formless void* is a word pair in Hebrew that only occurs in two other places (Jeremiah 4:23 and Isaiah 34:11). Whatever the exact meaning of this phrase may be, it would appear that one aspect of chaos is the absence of all structure. (2) The Hebrew word for "the face of the waters" (*Tehom*) is a proper name, which refers to the primeval waters. These waters are at the core of creation and in heaven. Although biblical writers do not want to give these waters a personality (and thus make them divine), nevertheless, these waters have a threatening quality that borders on personality. In Babylonian religion the primeval waters are, in fact, a goddess, *Tiamat*—a word somewhat similar to the Hebrew in this verse, *Tehom*. The word for darkness also has a threatening quality. (3) Finally the reference to the "wind from God" is also ambiguous, since this word can function as a superlative and thus mean "a mighty wind," rather than a wind from God.

The ambiguity of syntax and of the language in Genesis 1:1-2 cautions us about being too overconfident in our interpretations of the primeval forces within creation. One suspects that the ambiguity is intentional because of the subject matter. Yet several conclusions do rise to the surface. At the heart of creation is dark water, which, without the structure of creation, is threatening. Two analogies may provide insight into the threatening character of v. 2. One is the contemporary theory concerning black holes, with their ability to suck all light into themselves. They are not divine, but they are the opposite of what we would call a stable creation, and, as such, they provide insight into darkness. Second, the catastrophe of the *Exxon Valdez* in Alaskan waters provides insight into the threatening aspect of the dark primeval waters, which when let loose can destroy everything in its wake.

"Uncreated" matter is like the combination of an oil slick and a black hole. We humans could not regenerate in or survive the experience of either a black hole or an oil slick.

Genesis 1:1-5 adds a chilling aspect to our reflection of baptism. It underscores how water is both necessary for life but also threatening. The point of the text, however, is not to create terror, but to illustrate the creative power of God. Verses 3-5 make this point by showing how God can create structure and stability out of this unruly material. The creation of light to contrast with darkness is simply the first in a series of contrasts that result in the delicate balance of creation that we experience in our day to day lives. Genesis 1:1-5 provides an important dimension to our reflection on baptism, for it takes this rite outside of a community experience and places it in the larger context of mythology, that is the relationship of God to the entire world.

The Response: *Psalm 29*

God Rules the Floods

Setting. Psalm 29 is an ancient hymn of praise, which has taken elements of Canaanite worship. It celebrates the rule of God over nature through the motifs of a storm. Thus the "voice of the Lord" (which occurs seven times in vv. 3-9) is best interpreted as thunder. The imagery of the storm moves from the northern region of Israel through to the south. For further discussion of Psalm 29 see the Baptism of the Lord, Year A.

Structure. Psalm 29 follows the three-part structure of the hymn. It begins with an introduction in vv. 1-2, which call the worshipers to praise God. The body of the hymn consists of vv. 3-9, which recount the praiseworthy actions of God. Verses 10-11 provide a conclusion by providing the reason why God is praiseworthy.

Significance. The power of God over water is certainly the most striking aspect of the hymn in light of the motif of watery chaos in Genesis 1:1-5. In vv. 3-9 the psalm celebrates the power of God to control the thunderstorm on earth. The psalmist tells us that the voice or thunder of God is evident in the storm both over the water and the land. The psalm also celebrates the power of God to control primeval water in vv. 10-11. The image in the conclusion is that God is king of creation and thus enthroned over the flood. The Hebrew word for flood, *mabbul*, in v. 10 refers to the heavenly waters, which requires comment. Had our interpretation of Genesis 1 continued into the second day (vv. 6-8), it would have become apparent that once the opposite of darkness was created in day one by the interjection of light, God turned his attention to the chaotic waters in order to tame them by splitting them in half with a firmament or dome. As a result of this splitting there was water above the dome and below the dome. The *mabbul* waters result from this splitting, for they signify the heavenly waters above the dome. Even though they are split they can be very chaotic. In fact, it is these waters that pour out of heaven to cause the flood in Genesis 7:11.

Notice how the psalm follows the central questions of mythology in vv. 10-11. The description of God and the relationship of God to the world provides definition for the worshiping community in the following way. The reference to the enthronement of God over the *mabbul* (v. 10) allows the psalm to end on a note of confidence for the worshiping community (v. 11). Thus the final verse is a confession that because God can control any chaos in creation, God can surely bless and give peace to the people of God. This conclusion is surely the central point for preaching both Genesis 1:1-5 and Psalm 29.

New Testament Texts

The passage from Acts recalls the encounter of Paul in Ephesus with certain disciples of John the Baptist and how they came to full Christian discipleship. The Gospel lesson focuses on the person and work of the Baptist and, then, tells of the appearance of Jesus and of his baptism by John. John, Jesus, baptism, and the Spirit are the unifying elements of these two otherwise disparate texts. A sermon that seeks to deal with both lessons (always a difficult effort) could treat the themes of prophecy, fulfillment, submission, and empowerment.

The Epistle: *Acts 19:1-7*

The Knowledge and Experience of Christ

Setting. Acts 18:18–19:41 recalls the ministry of Paul and his associates in Ephesus. In telling of this time, Luke (the author of Acts) presents a series of peculiar religious personalities: (1) Apollos who was capable of accurate teaching, though he had not received Christian baptism and was in need of additional instruction; (2) disciples of John the Baptist who knew nothing of the Holy Spirit and who underwent baptism in the name of the Lord Jesus; (3) some "itinerant Jewish exorcists" who healed by pronouncing the name of the Lord Jesus, though they were not themselves believers; (4) many believers who continued to practice magic despite their discipleship; and (5) devotees of Artemis who opposed the Christians because of social and economic interests. Our lesson focuses on the second of these figures or groups.

Structure. The story is a model of evangelism and a lesson about the ultimately theological character of conversion. Paul's initial interaction with the "disciples" of John the Baptist exposes and addresses their lack of knowledge. Paul finds these people; he converses with them and learns of their ignorance of the Holy Spirit; and he instructs them about the fulfillment of John's prophecy in Jesus. In turn, the story shows us how these disciples' lack of religious experience was remedied. They are baptized in the name of the Lord Jesus, Paul lays hands on them, the Holy Spirit comes upon them, and they speak in tongues and prophesy. Lack of knowledge and lack of experience are dealt with in this story.

Significance. The story is a paradigm for dealing with deficient forms of faith. The designation of the persons Paul encounters in this story as "disciples" gives us a quick, firm impression that turns out to be false. These people do not prove to be false disciples, they are not disciples—despite the language used to name them. As folk called disciples, but who are not, they demonstrate the terrible truth that a little knowledge is often worse than no knowledge at all. Thinking they are one thing, they prove to be quite another; although had their self-designation been taken at face value no one would have perceived the deficiency of their faith.

In exposing this problem the story does not issue an invitation to launch a new grand inquisition to test the orthodoxy of the faith of others; rather, the story shows us a positive way of dealing with clearly faulty faith. In Luke's time, as in all of Christian history, there are persons whose Christian knowledge and experience are inadequate. We need not cry, "Heretic!" upon encountering such persons, for they may well not be enemies of the faith; instead, we should follow the lead of Paul and work with these people in order to bring them to adequate knowledge and experience. Discipleship can have a faulty start, but we should not conclude that inadequate conditions must remain ever unchanged. Christian instruction brings sound knowledge and leads to vital experience.

Having met these persons, having told them of the fulfillment of God's work in Jesus Christ, having moved with them through baptism, and having laid on hands, Paul has been faithful to his commission to ministry. Indeed, he has done what was humanly possible (of course, with divine aid). Now, the story reminds us in a powerful way that the real work of conversion, of the transformation of a human life into the life of discipleship, actually comes by the operation of God's Spirit. It is the power and the presence of the Holy Spirit in the lives of these persons that translates their experience beyond the mechanics of human religion to the dynamic level of divine reality. The leadership and power of the Spirit moves these baptized and confirmed believers to enthusiastic utterance and even prophecy; so that as they are made true members of the community of disciples they become active in the ministry to which they were called and which they have experienced.

In reflecting on this lesson for preaching one may ponder the necessity of a well-informed and spiritually dynamic faith, the appropriate Christian response to inadequate faith, the necessity of honest exchange in sharing the faith, and the dependability and authority of God in the work of evangelization and growth in faith. The tone of this account is mysterious but positive. We will do well to remember that the reality of faith is indeed a mystery. We are not called to judge and to condemn others in relation to faith. We are commissioned to share the gospel with all, knowing that persons of faith will hear the good news with joy, and trusting that the Spirit will enrich those whose faith is deficient so that they may experience the vitality of faith.

The Gospel: *Mark 1:4-11*

Baptism and the Holy Spirit

Setting. Mark 1:1-8 was the lesson for the Second Sunday of Advent, so the following commentary is in part a repetition of that entry. Since the 1950s interpreters tend to view Mark 1:1-13 (some even argue for 1:1-15) as a multifaceted prologue or introduction to the Gospel. The lectionary's selection of Mark 1:4-11 comes from the heart of that unit and gives us a portion of the text that commentators universally agree is introductory material.

Structure. Having explained the significance of John the Baptist's activity (1:1-3), the prologue to Mark continues by telling of the character of John's ministry (v. 4), of the popular response to his work (v. 5), and then of John's striking appearance (v. 6). Verses 7-8 report the content of John's preaching. A sermon might ponder, "What is the meaning of the gospel?" And, following the text, the answers come: It is the fulfillment of God's promises; it is God's reaching out through faithful witnesses to humanity in a most striking way; it is most specifically God's work in God's Son, Jesus Christ; and it has as its focus and content the very person of Jesus. In turn, vv. 9-11 recount the appearance of Jesus and the events around his baptism by John.

Significance. All the wonderful and interesting information about John the Baptist in the prologue to Mark's Gospel should not lure us into major meditation on the person and the work of the Baptist. Mark makes clear that John is a forerunner, and as such he holds a high place in God's fulfillment of the promise of salvation. But John is not the Messiah. Rather he points to another, greater than he, who is both the focus of our attention in this Gospel, and, as believers, the object of our devotion. It is Jesus Christ who issues the baptism in the Holy Spirit— namely, the power and presence of the saving grace of God. As the story progresses we learn that Jesus is the one who baptizes with the Holy Spirit precisely because the very Spirit of God rested upon him in his life and ministry. Thus, as we know him, we know God and the power of God's Spirit, and we come to understand ourselves. We are able to focus on Jesus Christ and form a theology which has sufficient content and precision to allow us, in turn—but only in turn—to develop an anthropology, our understanding of human nature and behavior, which is theologically sound. Then we can say that Jesus lives within us, or that we have the mind of Christ.

The vision Jesus experiences and the voice he hears from heaven make clear that he is the divinely appointed, divinely anointed, and divinely affirmed Son of God. This conviction is the heart of Mark's Gospel; above all he believes and is intent to teach the reader that Jesus is the Son of God. Yet a sermon cannot simply shout that Jesus is the Son of God. Even if we agree that this declaration is true, what exactly does it mean to say that Jesus Christ is the Son of God? Mark's intent in the Gospel is a deliberate effort to define the title, "Son of God." He instructs the reader of the Gospel on the meaning of this title by playing it off against another, "Son of Man." Through the course of the Gospel, prior to his death on the cross, only supernatural forces—God and the demons—actually recognize that Jesus is the Son of God. To all others Jesus presents himself and steadily refers to himself as the Son of Man. We come to comprehend who Jesus Christ is as the Son of God only when we follow him through this Gospel as the Son of Man. Who then is the Son of Man? From a reading of the Gospel we can say that Jesus, the Son of Man, is the one who does God's will and God's work in battling the forces of evil for the salvation of humankind. Above all, Jesus, the Son of Man, is the one who dies on the cross, giving his life on behalf of humanity for humanity's salvation. Thus Jesus the Son of God is God's selfless servant who gives even himself to save others! Jesus, the Son of God, makes provision for the salvation of humanity. He reveals with utter clarity the depth of God's love and the essential, selfless, serving nature of God. And Jesus, the Son of God, shows human beings the manner of life to which God calls us all.

EPIPHANY 1 (THE BAPTISM OF THE LORD): THE CELEBRATION

The celebration of Jesus' baptism on the First Sunday After Epiphany is patterned after the practice of the Eastern church and reminds us that it is his baptism that inaugurates our Lord's ministry in all the Gospels. We are called by this commemoration to remember our own baptisms and examine once more how faithful we have been to our call to follow Christ. The renewal of baptismal vows can be significant following a sermon that has dealt with the relationship of baptism to the work of ministry. Both sermon and liturgy should emphasize that the ministry under discussion is Christ's ministry, not ours or even the Church's, lest the enterprise degenerate into a celebration of our own good intentions and an orgy of goal setting. An alternative to the renewal of baptismal vows can be the use of water as a sign of forgiveness after a general confession of sin. Water from the font might be sprinkled towards the people while the minister uses a formula such as the following from I Corinthians 6:11:

> You were washed,
> you were sanctified,
> you were justified
> in the name of the Lord Jesus Christ
> and in the Spirit of our God.
> Remember your baptisms with thanksgiving
> and rejoice that your sin has been blotted out.

Today is one of the major days in the Christian year for the administration of holy baptism because it provides an opportunity to relate our baptism to Christ's and to emphasize that, as with Christ, our baptism is the beginning of our ministry. Established times for baptism in the local congregation (as opposed to "baptism on demand") is that it makes clear that baptism is a significant communal event with theological content that is rooted in the biblical narrative. Today's lessons become even more vivid within the context of the administration of baptism.

Liturgical presiders who are doing both baptisms and a reaffirmation of baptism should think carefully about the amount of water used in each event. If the people are sprinkled at reaffirmation, then much more water should be used for the actual baptisms in order to have the signs clearly distinguished and not give the impression that the reaffirmation is some kind of re-baptism. Where immersions are not possible for baptisms, then a generous pouring should be employed. If at all possible, arrange the setting for the baptism so that the water can be seen and heard by as many as possible.

St. Gregory of Nazianzus (late-fourth century), in one of his sermons, makes clear how today's Old Testament lesson is related to the theme of Jesus' baptism and ours, because he understands baptism to be a type of the new creation:

> John is baptizing when Jesus draws near. Perhaps he comes to sanctify his baptizer; certainly he comes to bury sinful humanity in the waters. He comes to sanctify the Jordan for our sake and in readiness for us; he who is spirit and flesh comes to begin a new creation through the Spirit and water.
>
> Jesus rises from the waters; the world rises with him. The heavens like Paradise with its flaming sword, closed by Adam for himself and his descendants, are rent open. (*Christian Prayer: The Liturgy of the Hours* [Baltimore: Helicon Press, 1976], pp. 1760-61)

The color for today continues to be white or gold. "Hail to the Lord's Anointed" is an appropriate hymn for this day because of its emphasis on Jesus' ministry. The recognition of the Baptism of the Lord as a special day in the Church's calendar has produced several new hymns. Among these are:

"Anointed of God, How Can We See You" (United Church of Christ hymnal)

"Christ, When for Us You Were Baptized" (Episcopal and Presbyterian hymnals)

"I Come, the Great Redeemer Cries" (Episcopal)

"Lord, When You Came to Jordan" (Presbyterian)

"The Sinless One to Jordan Came" (Episcopal)

"When Jesus Came to Jordan" (Presbyterian and United Methodist)

"When Jesus Went to Jordan's Stream" (Episcopal, and in the Lutheran hymnal as "To Jordan Came the Christ, Our Lord")

Second Sunday After Epiphany

Old Testament Texts

Second Samuel 3 is the account of Samuel's call in the Temple, when he is living with the prophetic priest, Eli. Psalm 139:1-6, 13-18 is a hymn of praise to the omnipresent God.

The Lesson: *I Samuel 3:1-10 (11-20)*

God's Initiative

Setting. The Song of Hannah in I Samuel 2:1-8 provides an introduction to the thematic and structural development for I and II Samuel. A brief look at this hymn provides background for reading the lectionary text. The book opens with a conflict between Hannah, who is barren, and Peninnah, who has many children. This story is familiar and can be summarized quickly. Hannah goes to Shiloh and prays for a child at the sanctuary where Eli is priest. Her request is for a son, which God grants in the birth of Samuel. Hannah's song celebrates the power of God to answer prayer and to initiate salvation. The content of her song is very important, for she describes the power of God to initiate salvation as radical reversals in life. God can bring the arrogant low and break the bows of the mighty (vv. 2-4*a*), and, conversely, he can strengthen the weak and feed the hungry (vv. 4*b*-5*a*). Finally, Hannah celebrates the reversal in her own life by recounting God's power to make a barren woman pregnant (v. 5*b*). The song underscores how God's ability to initiate salvation is a two-sided sword: "he brings low, he also exalts" (v. 7*b*). The thematic development of I and II Samuel is in many ways an illustration of Hannah's song. Characters are frequently paired in contrasting situations, so that while one is on the rise, another is on the decline (Peninnah versus Hannah, Eli [and his sons] versus Samuel, Samuel [and his sons] versus

111

Saul, Saul [and his sons] versus David, etc.). This structure provides background for reading the call of Samuel in I Samuel 3.

Structure. The interrelationship of characters is central to the story, and, for that reason, it is important to include the larger boundaries of the lectionary text, vv. 1-20. The text separates into four parts: vv. 1-3 provide an introduction and setting, vv. 4-9 are an introductory word for the call of Samuel, vv. 10-15 are the account of God's revelation, and vv. 16-20 provide the conclusion. Note how the story begins (vv. 1-3) and ends (vv. 16-20) with Eli and Samuel, while the two middle sections focus primarily on Samuel and God.

Significance. The central focus for the lectionary is God's initiative. This topic is central to John 1:43-51, and it is the reason why the call of Samuel has been inserted into this Sunday. The call of Samuel is a good choice for this Sunday, because it adds complexity to our too easy confessions about God's initiative in our lives, especially during good times. More specifically, it is the character of Eli that adds complexity to the story, and our interpretation will focus on the important (and ambiguous) role that he plays in bringing the call of Samuel to a proper conclusion.

As noted, Samuel and Eli frame the story of I Samuel 3. We should also note, however, that by the time we reach the conclusion their roles are reversed. In the introduction we are told that Samuel is a mere boy and that he is serving Eli. Furthermore, we learn that although God is removed ("the word of the Lord was rare in those days"), he is not completely absent, because of Eli (Eli's eyesight is dim but "the lamp of God had not yet gone out."). This statement in v. 2 has several functions in the larger story. On the one hand the reference to dimness prepares us for the rise of Samuel and the fall of Eli. On the other hand, it makes Eli an ambiguous character, because he still has "sight." The earlier chapter introduced this ambiguity concerning Eli through the story of his worthless sons (2:22-25). Yet Eli is not his sons, and even though they reflect a flaw in him, he is still a priest of God. This situation raises the question of how he will act in his own decline.

God enters the story in the two middle sections. With clever repetition, God addresses Samuel three times (vv. 4-9) before the boy understands his own clairvoyance at the fourth intervention (vv. 10-15). We can read these sections as the call of Samuel, and if we do so, the story illustrates the power of God to initiate salvation even to a child. But such a reading is too simplistic, because it is the dim vision of Eli that is the real catalyst for God's initiative. Note how in v. 7 we are explicitly told that Samuel did not know God. Then in v. 8 it is Eli who perceives the call of God, and in v. 9 he tutors the boy on how to respond to God. Eli's tutoring of Samuel allows the revelation in vv. 10-15 to take place, which, paradoxically, is a judgment against Eli. The judgment is so severe that the ears of anyone who hears it will actually tingle (v. 11, see also II Kings 21:12 and Habakkuk 3:16 for further discussion of "tingling" because of divine judgment).

God is once again absent in the conclusion. It begins in v. 15 with the relationship between Samuel and Eli unchanged. Samuel fears to convey the message, but Eli exerts his authority by invoking a potential divine curse on the boy (v. 17). Thus Samuel capitulates and tells the priest of his downfall. Eli is given the final words of this exchange ("It is the LORD; let him do what seems good to him."), before he exits the story altogether, signifying the reversal in the roles between Samuel and Eli.

This is an insightful story for preaching on the topic of God's initiative, for it complicates our understanding of divine action. To focus exclusively on the call of the disciples in John 1, or the call of Samuel in I Samuel 3 runs the danger of being too romantic. The call of God then becomes illustrative of good things happening to good people. In preaching this text it is important to show how the disciples and Samuel also live in the grey and ambiguous world of Eli, where the real challenge of confessing God's power is when it may imply our own downfall. Biblical writers have underscored this point by making Eli such an important character in the call of Samuel, who, himself, will be in Eli's place within several chapters.

The Response: *Psalm 139:1-6, 13-18*

A Hymn of Praise

Setting. The categorization of Psalm 139 as a hymn of praise is in fact not so clear. There is a didactic quality to Psalm 139, in which the psalmist draws from the wisdom tradition about creation and appears to teach those around her about the omnipresence of God, while the end of the psalm actually becomes a lament. The reason for designating the psalm as a hymn is to avoid the danger of reading this litany of divine power and presence as though it were impersonal. The content of the psalm arises out of the experience of the psalmist, who makes the statement about the absolute control of God over all time and space a source of praise. This is not a psalm that explores the dialectic of freedom and necessity.

Structure. The larger structure of Psalm 139 separates into two parts: vv. 1-18 are a hymn and vv. 19-24 are a lament. The shift in mood between these two sections is so sharp that a number of scholars have argued for two separated psalms. This may in fact be the case. The only problem with this conclusion is the close tie between vv. 1 and 23.

The lectionary reading is a portion of the first part of the hymn. Verses 1-18 separate into three parts: vv. 1-6 are a confession of how intimately God knows the psalmist, vv. 7-12 reflect on the omnipresence of God through creation, while vv. 13-18 continue the reflection by moving to the more intimate metaphors of how God was present in the creation of the psalmist.

Significance. We grasp the central point of this hymn by discerning the combination of outer and inner space in vv. 7-12 and 13-17. Verses 7-12 underscore how God is everywhere by showing how the psalmist cannot escape the spirit in either heaven or hell (vv. 7-8), in the farthermost reaches of the sea (vv. 9-10), or even through magical incantations of conjuring up darkness (vv. 11-12). Such conceptions of omnipresence could be terrifying, but we spring into praise through the change in the direction of images from the outer reaches of cosmology in vv. 7-12 to the intimacy of the psalmist's own creation in vv. 13-18. The imagery of God's presence in the privacy of the mother's womb in v. 13 may be anatomical, but it is more likely a reference to the earth. Note how v. 15 continues the imagery of v. 13 and explicitly states that the place of secret formation is the depths of the earth. In either case the point of this imagery is that the omnipresence of God is at the very origin of our creation. God has even beheld our unformed substance (v. 16), hence there is really nothing left to hide. The psalmist concludes from this that God's presence is not something to be avoided or feared, but embraced, even when we cannot imagine how, or in what ways, our life's journey interweaves with God (v. 18). One is reminded faintly at the end of this psalm (v. 18, "I am still with you") of Eli and his closing comments in I Samuel 3:18: "It is the Lord; let him do what seems good to him."

New Testament Texts

The passage from I Corinthians is the first of several sequential readings from Paul's letter to the congregation in Corinth. The passage from the gospel according to John takes a step beyond the focus of last week's Gospel lesson, in part about John the Baptist (from Mark's Gospel), by recounting how some of the Baptist's disciples became followers of Jesus.

The Epistle: *I Corinthians 6:12-20*

The Meaning of Christian Freedom

Setting. Paul's letter to the church in Corinth addresses that congregation about a variety of concerns, all of which are related to the desire of the members of the church to boast of their spiritual superiority. Chapters 5 and 6 form the second major portion of the body of the letter, addressing two broad issues that have been reported to Paul: (1) judging and dealing with immoral behavior in the context of the church and (2) determining what is "permissible" activity for Christians. Our lesson comes in the course of Paul's remarks in relation to the second of these themes.

Structure. This is a complex section of the letter, containing quotations from the Corinthians themselves, a citation of the Old Testament, and perhaps a line from Paul's own teaching. These various items are used in conjunction with Paul's argument. The lesson has two distinguishable sections: vv. 12-17 build and argue a case in response to a position taken by the Corinthians, and vv. 18-20 direct the recipients of the letter to shun immorality because their body is the temple of the Holy Spirit. It is crucial in working to develop a sermon from this text to follow Paul's logic through the two larger sections, not so much to reproduce the pattern of his thoughts as to remain consistently in dialogue with his purposes and points.

Significance. Throughout this whole lesson Paul verbally jabs at the Corinthians, "Don't you know . . . Don't you know . . . Don't you know . . . ?" Obviously they don't! Paul contends they ought to know better than to live as they do, so he tells them what they should know in order to modify their behavior.

The first portion of the passage (vv. 12-17) is cast in the form of a diatribe, a style of popular Hellenistic philosophical argumentation wherein one quotes and argues against an imaginary opponent. We hear Paul quoting the Corinthians who say, "All things are lawful for me." In turn, Paul answers, "But not all things are beneficial." Again, we hear from the Corinthians, "All things are lawful for me"; to which Paul replies, "But I will not be dominated by anything."

Literally rendered the Corinthians' slogan says, "All things to me are permissible." Anyone who has read Paul's own letters—for example, Galatians 5:1a, "For freedom Christ has set us free"—can believe that the Corinthians may have learned their slogan from the apostle himself. Notice how Paul allows the correctness of the slogan but, here, qualifies it! For the Corinthians, what they knew had given them an abstract principle that could and did produce less than desirable results. In order to combat the problem Paul concretizes Christian freedom. Freedom, he insists, is characterized by pursuing what is best, and Christian freedom does not lead to a new form of slavery.

The Corinthians claim an inner freedom that places them above the mundane realities of the world. They apparently delight in demonstrating this freedom in their outlandish behavior in relation to food and sexual activity. Paul's critique of the abuse of freedom calls the Corinthians into a responsible relationship to "the Lord." In 6:16b-17 the apostle quotes Genesis 2:24, first, to denounce involvement with prostitutes and, second, to set up an explanation of the nature of spiritual union of the Christian(s) with the Lord.

Verses 18-20 inform the Corinthians of the limits of their freedom. Believers are not purely independent in their freedom. Why? Because, as Paul says, they were bought with a price. The apostle teaches that freedom comes through redemption. The metaphor here is that of a ransom, and Paul employs it as a loose undeveloped traditional image. Paul's point is this: Christians belong to God, and that relationship is the ultimate qualification of freedom.

How do we abuse God's grace today? How are we spiritually smug? Are there patterns in our living that we believe demonstrate our own superior spirituality? Is our "easy" attitude toward discipleship as destructive in its passivity ("Smile, God loves you" or "Saved by faith, not works" or "It doesn't really matter what you believe as long as you believe it with all your heart") as was the bizarre activity of the Corinthians?

The Gospel: *John 1:43-51*

"Come and See"

Setting. Following the testimony of John the Baptist that Jesus (1:29, 36) is the Lamb of God, we learn that two of John's disciples became followers of Jesus (1:37). In turn, one of the two, Andrew, called his brother, Simon Peter (1:40-42). Our lesson continues the story of the calling of the disciples, first, by recalling Jesus' calling of Philip and, then, by recounting Philip's recruiting of Nathanael which leads to an exchange between Jesus and Nathanael.

It is instructive to compare the call of the disciples in the Fourth Gospel with the parallel accounts in the Synoptic Gospels, for there are noticeable differences concerning where, whom, how, and in what order the disciples were called. It seems clear, however, and historical that the first disciples were followers of John the Baptist prior to becoming Jesus' companions, and it seems likely that the Fourth Gospel fills these scenes with far more theology than is to be associated with bare historical remembrance.

Structure. The passage "moves" through narrative sequential development. Jesus calls Philip. Philip calls Nathanael. Nathanael expresses reservations, but when he encounters Jesus he changes his mind and expresses confidence in Jesus. Finally, Jesus makes a statement that appears to be a prophetic pronouncement.

A sermon might deal with similar themes that develop progressively: We are moved to faith by a personal encounter with Jesus Christ; others learn of Jesus through our testimony; the reservations of others to our testimony are answered by Jesus himself; ultimately it is Jesus Christ who brings others to faith. The movement to faith is but the beginning of fuller perceptions of God's power at work through Jesus Christ.

Significance. As early as the first chapter of John, and continuing throughout the course of the Fourth Gospel, the evangelist recounts incidents and exchanges that individually present the entire Christian perception of truth about Jesus Christ. The verses of our lesson telescope the history of early Christian insights about the identity and significance of Christ into a moment of story time. The image we gain from the Synoptic Gospels and other early Christian literature is that the disciples and other early believers struggled slowly and steadily through the course of Jesus' ministry, through the time of his Passion, and even after the beginning of Resurrection-faith on Easter to grasp who and what Jesus Christ was in God's work for salvation. Yet, in the scene portrayed by our lesson, early in Jesus' ministry Philip and Nathanael recognize him as the prophet-like-Moses, Rabbi, the Son of God, and the King of Israel. The passage seeks to declare at once the gradually growing early Christian comprehension of Jesus, which increased from Teacher to Messiah to Son of God to King (an Old Testament image for God!).

The passage issues a call to discipleship. It presents in bold terms a striking early Christian range of convictions and claims about Jesus Christ. Yet, as we see in the story, the testimony of others—accurate though it is—is no more than an invitation to personal involvement with Jesus Christ. Discipleship is never based merely on hearsay. We humans, as disciples, are no more or less than witnesses to our Lord. We call others to discipleship, which is actually based on more than our words. We speak of Jesus Christ, perhaps arousing curiosity or even doubts in those to whom we bear witness; but the work of conviction and the ultimate call to discipleship is for others what it is for us— namely, a new reality issuing from genuine personal encounter with Jesus Christ. The call may come initially through testimony, but it is founded and grows through authentic experience of the power of God at work in and through Jesus Christ. Discipleship is always a current and present reality, and it also always has about it a strong future dimension. God's work in Jesus Christ is real right now, but it is not exhausted in the present. God's work has begun in Jesus Christ, and the promise to those who "come and see" and, thereby, come to see—that is, to believe—is that the future holds an even greater display of God's power. Thus the call to discipleship is not only to "come and see," but once seeing through an encounter with Christ, to keep eyes wide open looking for what God is about in the world.

EPIPHANY 2: THE CELEBRATION

The time after Epiphany, with its emphasis on the light that has broken upon the world in Jesus Christ, provides a liturgical occasion for the use of Prayers for Illumination to introduce the reading of the lessons and the sermon. These may be the same as the Opening Prayer or the Collect for the day, but if they are designated "Prayer for Illumination," then some reference to light should be featured in the prayer. One or more of the lessons may provide the basis for the prayer, as in the following from today's propers:

> Lighten our darkness, faithful God,
> by the lamp of your word;
> and though our faith be dim,
> open our ears to hear your call
> and to follow your Son,
> Jesus of Nazareth.

Such prayers for illumination immediately prior to the lessons and the sermon are preferable to those prayers sometimes heard immediately before the sermon that often sound as though the preacher is doing his/her private devotions in public or trying to gain the congregation's sympathy and support. By placing the prayer before the lessons one identifies the reading and the preaching as part of the same corporate event. A collection of Prayers for Illumination is to be found in the *Presbyterian Supplemental Liturgical Resource 1, The Service for the Lord's Day* (Philadelphia: Westminster, 1984), pp. 59-61. The refrain of the hymn, "Open My Eyes, That I May See," may also serve as a sung Prayer for Illumination.

The Song of Hannah (I Samuel 2:1*b*-10), discussed above in the commentary on today's Old Testament lesson, may be used in place of Psalm 139 or as a canticle or responsive reading in its own right. If Hannah's Song is used as the response to the first lesson, then Psalm 139 might be employed as part of the entrance rite, possibly as a responsive call to worship using vv. 7-10. The same psalm could then be used as part of the conclusion of the service, with vv. 11-12 being used responsively followed by the singing of the third stanza of "Savior, Again to Thy Dear Name We Raise," with its last line based on Psalm 139:12. The formal benediction or blessing would follow.

Third Sunday After Epiphany

Old Testament Texts

Jonah 3:1-5, 10 is the account of how the prophet Jonah proclaimed judgment on Nineveh, while Psalm 62:5-12 is a call to trust in God.

The Lesson: *Jonah 3:1-5, 10*

Missing the Point

Setting. Jonah is a satirical book about an eighth century prophet, who is mentioned in passing in II Kings 14:25 as someone who prophesied in Northern Israel during the reign of Jeroboam II. The relationship between this prophet and the anti-hero of the book of Jonah is difficult to determine. The connection may be nationalism. The prophet Jonah in II Kings 14:25 appears to be a nationalistic prophet, since he is active at the time when Jeroboam II was establishing the boarders of the Northern Kingdom. There is no question that the character in the book of Jonah is also a nationalistic prophet, because it provides the background for satirical criticism.

The subject matter of the book of Jonah is grave and serious, but the events that unfold present a comedy of horrors. The story opens with God commanding Jonah to present a word of judgment against Nineveh, to which the prophet responds by fleeing. His flight leads him to board a ship traveling to Tarshish and eventually (with some divine intervention) into the stomach of a fish, whereupon the prophet bursts into song causing the fish to vomit him out. As if this is not enough, the whole story begins anew with the lectionary text, when God calls Jonah a second time in 3:1 to go to Nineveh. The point of the satire in the second half of the book revolves around the issue of repentance, which is also the central theme in Mark 1:14-20.

Structure. The lectionary text must be seen in the larger context of Jonah 3–4. The lectionary reading actually frames chapter 3 by including

vv. 1-5 and 10. These verses give the account of Jonah's announcement of divine judgment (v. 4), Nineveh's repentance (v. 5), as well as God's (v. 10). But the conversion of Nineveh does not end the story. Chapter 4 explores Jonah's anger over the fact that God's grace was offered to Nineveh in the first place, then his anger is compounded by their conversion. The thought of worshiping with the Ninevites is more than he can bear, which prompts his request for death.

Significance. The central theme of Jonah 3:1-5, 10 is repentance, and, as we have seen, it provides a complement to Mark 1:14-20 where Jesus inaugurates his ministry with the proclamation, "The time is fulfilled, and the kingdom of God has come near; repent, and believe the good news." In view of the explicit links between the Old Testament and Gospel lessons, perhaps the best way to interpret the theme of repentance in Jonah 3:1-5, 10 is as a counterpoint to Mark 1:14-20. The contrast is not between Judaism and Christianity, but between the universal call of repentance by Jesus and our desire to place boundaries on the limits of salvation. When viewed in this way, Jonah 3:1-5, 10 is an illustration of what not to do in preaching repentance, even though the prophet Jonah prompts one of the larger mass conversions in history.

A close look at Jonah 3:1-5, 10 reveals a series of very surprising if not absurd events. The first thing to notice is the message of Jonah. He makes no reference to God or to the fact that he is functioning as a prophet, which we would expect in such a situation, with the typical introduction, "Thus says the Lord. . . . " Furthermore, neither does he call Nineveh to repent nor does he even provide a moral judgment on their activity. He merely predicts the downfall of the city within forty days. As far as the Ninevites are concerned Jonah could be a geologist predicting the next tremor. The second peculiar aspect of the narrative is the mass conversion of Nineveh. We are told in v. 5 that they believed in God and called a fast. Such a mass conversion is unusual under any circumstances (especially for the Ninevites), but when we look at the announcement of doom by Jonah, it is a marvel, since the prophet has given no indication that God is the force behind his message. The third development in the text is the only event that follows a normal course. God sees the repentance of the Ninevites and in response changes his mind concerning their fate in v. 10.

The point of this text is not really the Ninevites, but Jonah and his reluctance to carry the grace of God beyond boundaries that he considered acceptable. Because of his prejudice, the satirical comedy moves to a potentially tragic ending when Jonah contemplates suicide (4:8). The story trails off, however, without a real ending, and we are left to fashion a conclusion. This lack of an ending certainly must be intentional on the part of the author, for it places us, the readers, into the character of Jonah, with the result that God's final question, "Should I not be concerned about Nineveh?" is one that we must answer in the present time. Jonah 3:1-5, 10 provides a good counterpart for preaching on Jesus' call for repentance in Mark 1:14-20 because it describes (1) how uncomfortable most of us are with the ideal of universal salvation and (2) how God works with us in spite of our prejudices.

The Response: *Psalm 62:5-12*

Trusting in God

Setting. Psalm 62:5-12 is a prayer song of an individual that focuses on trusting in God. The singer has most likely entered the sanctuary for asylum from persecutors, which prompts the song of trust. The psalm is somewhat peculiar when read as a response to Jonah 3:1-5, 10 because it certainly doesn't fit the prophet. He does not reach the point of trust at the end of the book. One way to read Psalm 62:5-12 is for the worshiping congregation to claim it as the ending of the book of Jonah. In this case, the psalm would become their answer to the question of whether God should in fact care about the Ninevites.

Structure. Psalm 62 separates into three parts: Verses 1-7 present a series of confessional statements by the psalmist about trusting in God (vv. 1-2, 5-7) even during times of persecution (vv. 3-4); vv. 8-10 shift the focus from the individual psalmist to the congregation when the psalmist encourages fellow worshipers to trust in God; and vv. 11-12 conclude the psalm by presenting a salvation oracle from God, which is providing the confidence that permeates the psalm. The lectionary text picks up the concluding verses of the first section (vv. 5-7), which does not really change the structure of the psalm. Much of the language in vv. 5-7 is a repetition from vv. 1-2. What has been eliminated, however, is the accusation of the psalmist in vv. 3-4 against his persecutors. Another way to read Psalm 62 is from the point of view of the Ninevites. In this case you may wish to include vv. 3-4, because they illustrate how Jonah was in fact their persecutor. From this point of view the psalm is self-criticism of the people of God.

Significance. The psalm is intended to be read backwards. What this means is that the salvation oracle in vv. 11-12 is the basis for all the language of trust in the earlier sections of the psalm. The divine oracle provides revelation about the character of God (1) as being powerful, (2) as having the quality of steadfast love, and finally, (3) as repaying humans in kind according to the quality of their work. The story of Jonah and the Ninevites provides illustration of these points in two different ways, for it, too, is meant to be a story about the steadfast love of God (Jonah 4:2). One aspect of steadfast love is God's ability to forgive even the sinful Ninevites, which is an illustration of the divine tendency to repay humans in kind. In this case human repentance prompts divine repentance. It is as though God modulates action in relation to humans. Another aspect of steadfast love is God's staying power with the people of God, even when we fail. God's persistence and constant tutoring of Jonah right up to the end of the book illustrates this quality. Trust is essential to both of these characteristics of divine steadfast love. Trusting that God is doing the right thing in forgiving the Ninevites is a challenge, even while trusting in God's staying power provides security. The message of the book of Jonah is that these are both the same quality. The psalmist is moving toward this same point with the exhortation in v. 8: "Trust in him at all times, O people; pour out your heart before him; God is a refuge for us."

New Testament Texts

The readings from I Corinthians continue and we find the first of several sequential readings from Mark as the Gospel lesson. The texts are very different, one being epistolary with hortatory concerns while the other is narrative with a combination of editorial, biographical, and didactic interests. Yet the passages are similar in their pronounced eschatological outlooks and motifs, betraying the radically eschatological cast of early Christian thought and life.

The Epistle: *I Corinthians 7:29-31*

Christian Living in the Present World

Setting. Chapters 7–10 of I Corinthians form the third major section of the body of the letter. Here, Paul begins to answer a series of questions that the Corinthians posed to him in a letter sent from Corinth to Paul in Ephesus. We can spot the questions asked of the apostle, for he introduces the Corinthians' concerns with such lines as, "Now concerning the matters about which you wrote . . . " and "Now concerning. . . . " Paul continues to restate the matters brought to his attention and to answer the queries throughout the remainder of the letter. These topics of concern are treated in distinguishable sections of the letter. Chapter 7, for example, is a unit of material dealing with celibacy, marriage, circumcision, and slavery—in other words, with the state and status of Christians in the world in the light of God's time.

Structure. These verses summarize and "cap off" Paul's remarks through the earlier portions of chapter 7, and they set the stage for the ensuing remarks in 7:32-40. In essence Paul says, (1) the time remaining before final judgment is brief; (2) therefore, believers are to live in freedom from preoccupation with the realities of this world; (3) because, the structures and substance of this world are already doing what they will soon do completely—namely, pass away.

Significance. These verses are a crucial passage in the writings of the apostle. He articulates a perspective on life in the world that results from his conviction about what God has done, is doing, and is about to do in and through Jesus Christ in relation to this world. To undervalue the importance of this text or to miss its point is disastrous, for valid comprehension of everything Paul said and did depends on understanding his work and teaching in terms of his eschatology.

In writing to the Corinthians Paul relativized everything with which the Corinthians seemed concerned by saying that this world and its present form are passing away. Paul's earlier remarks about sex, marriage, circumcision, slavery, and divorce are all related to his conviction that this world is coming to an end. The apostle instructs people to forget about expending energy changing their current social status—namely, single to married, slavery to freedom, or married to divorced. His social ethic appears to be disgustingly conservative, but only at a glance. Why does Paul advise against efforts at change? Because Paul was convinced that as God had acted in the cross of Christ, so God was about to act again at any moment in the coming of Christ. When Christ came, this world and all its structure would come under the transforming power of God's final judgment. And so, why bother to change something that was already set up to be eliminated? Why swim hard to get on a sinking ship? Why run to get aboard a derailed train? Why spend a fortune on a condemned house with no title to the land?

Paul's message is indeed one of radical freedom. In Jesus Christ God has declared the tentative nature of this world. In Jesus Christ God has revealed the promise of a transformed future, different from and independent of present structures and systems. For Paul the hope of the future is a confidence in the awesome, transforming power of God! Perceiving God's future granted Paul freedom from anxiety over this world and freedom for full dedication to "the affairs of the Lord" (7:32).

Paul's argument makes sense for us when we think in terms of circumcision, but when we examine his logic in relation to sex, marriage, slavery, and divorce, we have a more difficult time. Yet we must remember that Paul was genuinely convinced that Christ would probably come to effect God's final judgment before next Thursday. In fact, we do not share Paul's sense of eschatological urgency. With the passage of nearly 2000 years, we can hardly produce the apostle's outlook with any integrity.

What then should we do? Take Paul seriously! At the heart of this message is the liberating news that the structures of this world do not have the eternal blessing of God. God does not guarantee the status quo of worldly reality, and in Jesus Christ God has declared that this world is inadequate, unacceptable, and condemned. God's promise is to replace this flawed world-order with one free from problems. We can take this message as a form of pessimism, if we are primarily concerned with this world, but we can see Paul's position as inherently optimistic if we focus, as he did, on God and God's work in Christ which means freedom. Sermons in relation to this passage may refer to Paul's imprecise conviction of the imminent end of the world, but a more positive use of his thinking will focus on the supremacy of God over world-order and the freedom we have in Christ in relation to this world—freedom that actually means we may, can, and should work to make the world more like the one God promises for the future.

The Gospel: *Mark 1:14-20*

Called In and Out of the Present

Setting. Mark 1:1-11 forms a kind of prologue to the story of Jesus' ministry. Then, 1:12-13, recalls an interlude between the time of the ministry of John the Baptist and the beginning of Jesus' own public work. Our lesson recalls the launching of Jesus' ministry and begins to tell of Jesus' words and deeds.

Structure. The passage has two parts, vv. 14-15 and vv. 16-20. Scholars conclude these were originally independent memories in the life of the church. The first unit locates Jesus' ministry in time and place, and it gives a capsule version of Jesus' line of preaching. The second set of verses tells the story of the initial calling of principal disciples. A sermon can focus on either part of the lesson, or if ambitious, address both portions of the text.

Significance. Jesus' preaching has a pronounced eschatological tone: he declares that the time is fulfilled and the kingdom of God is at hand. This proclamation declares that God has now taken definitive action that demands attention. To say that "the time is fulfilled" is a roundabout way of saying that God had appointed the present moment as the time in which God is taking conclusive action. This thoroughgoing eschatology has profound implications for our lives right now, but we must not reduce this outlook to a mere "realized eschatology." The future is not swallowed up in the present, and the sense of expectation is not replaced by a declaration of real experience. God acts now so that God's action crashes into the course of human existence, placing powerful demands on our lives, but we are called forward into an existence that is qualitatively different from the life we are presently living. God's future beckons us in and out of the present into a life that is as yet unrealized and, in a sense, unknown.

Jesus' demand for repentance is remarkable. He does not say, "Repent so the kingdom can come" or "Repent before the kingdom comes." Rather, his words, "The kingdom of God has come near; repent . . . ," may be paraphrased, "Repent because the kingdom has come near." In other words, God's action in bringing forth the kingdom is the cause, the motivation for repentance. Humans do not enable God's action, but God's action demands human action. God's lordship over creation is exercised as God acts determinatively in relation to our world.

Furthermore, Jesus' words, "Repent, and believe in the good news," reveal the two related dimensions of the action that God demands. Repentance, as is well-known, is a turning from that which is wrong and contrary to God's will. But the mere cessation of incorrect living does not exhaust the will of God for our lives. We are called to belief, to a life of faith. We recant from godless living in order to take up a godly style of life, specifically one devoted to the embodiment of the standards of God's kingdom.

The second portion of our lesson shows Jesus calling his first disciples. Simon, Andrew, James, and John do not repent of fishing, they turn away from it, and as they believe the good news they become full-fledged disciples of Jesus Christ who are devoted to proclamation of the gospel in the manner of their master. When Jesus calls these fishermen to discipleship, he calls them above all to become followers. They are to move forward in the footsteps of Jesus. They are to travel in directions that he establishes. They are to subordinate their own wills to his, for he is the leader and they are his followers. Over and over throughout the remainder of Mark's account we will see the disciples fail in their calling precisely because they insist on taking over the lead. As the disciples try to tell Jesus the direction he should take, the manner in which he should lead them, they lapse from discipleship into actual opposition to God's work through Jesus Christ (see especially 8:22–10:52).

In this story, however, the four fishermen are models of discipleship. When called they follow without hesitation. They give up their former ways of life, even leaving behind the security of employment, family, and friends. They become disciples at a real price, ultimately giving their allegiance to the Lord and not seeking safety in the structures of this world.

EPIPHANY 3: THE CELEBRATION

This Sunday will frequently fall during the Week of Prayer for Christian Unity (January 18-25). Hymns and prayers should be chosen with that theme in mind, and the propers may be read in that light. What has Jonah to say about restrictive ecclesiastical systems that follow various kinds of lineage in preference to grace? What does it mean to be sheltered by the vine of our heritage with no appreciation for the giver of the vine? Does the freedom of which Paul speaks apply to the Church in its attempt to achieve a unified witness in the world? Do we make little progress in our ecumenical endeavors because we are enslaved to our individual systems and because we are fearful of a freedom that would break them open and leave us trusting only in God for the shape of things to come? What place does repentance have in the Church as we seek to realize the Good News and as we leave the old secure ways to answer Christ's call? To what degree is the Church itself an eschatological sign of what God intends for the whole creation?

Many communities provide for a series of ecumenical services during the Week of Prayer for Christian Unity. Even if this is not the case, pastors and congregations might plan an exchange of pulpits and/or choirs on this Sunday. Other representatives of the congregations can be encouraged to participate in the exchange as well.

Today's Gospel lesson suggests the use of "Dear Lord and Father of Mankind," or, to avoid the male imagery of the first stanza, the second stanza alone ("In simple trust like theirs who heard") may be used as a response to the reading of the Gospel lesson. "Jesus Calls Us" also draws upon the Markan narrative for its theme.

The following text by Charles Wesley is a fitting response to the lesson from Jonah because of its expression of the universal character of God's forgiveness. A long meter tune such as Melcombe or Pentecost may be used.

Father, whose everlasting love
Thy only Son for sinners gave,
Whose grace to all did freely move,
And sent him down the world to save.

Help us thy mercy to extol,
Immense, unfathomed, unconfined;
To praise the Lamb who died for all,
The general Savior of mankind.

Thy undistinguishing regard
Was cast on Adam's fallen race;
For all thou hast in Christ prepared
Sufficient, sovereign, saving grace.

The world he suffered to redeem;
For all he has the atonement made;
For those that will not come to him
The ransom of his life was paid.

Arise, O God, maintain thy cause!
The fullness of the nations call;
Lift up the standard of thy cross,
And all shall own thou diedst for all.

Fourth Sunday After Epiphany

Old Testament Texts

Deuteronomy 18:15-20 describes the role of the prophet in the community of faith. Psalm 111 is a hymn of praise celebrating the works of God and encouraging the community to fear God.

The Lesson: *Deuteronomy 18:15-20*

A Prophet Like Moses

Setting. Deuteronomy 18:15-20 is part of Moses' final address to Israel before he dies and the Israelites enter the land of Canaan. In the present passage Moses describes what the role of the prophet should be for Israel, and he predicts the rise of a prophet like himself. The prophet-like-Moses is applied to Jesus in Acts 3:22-23, which has given Deuteronomy 18:15-20 a messianic interpretation in Christian tradition. Our aim is to bracket the messianic interpretation in order to raise the question of what it means to be a prophet in the light of Deuteronomy 18:15-20. In addressing this question we will be in a better position, on the one hand, to understand why New Testament writers applied this text to Jesus, and, on the other hand, to determine what is its present significance.

Structure. The lectionary text must be interpreted in the larger context of Deuteronomy 18, which addresses the role of priest and prophet in ancient Israel. This chapter begins by outlining the role of the Levitical priest in vv. 1-8. The second half of the chapter focuses on the role of the prophet in vv. 9-22. Verses 9-14 outline aspects of prophecy that are not allowed in Israel. Verses 15-18 describe the proper actions of a prophet. Verses 19-22 address the problem of true and false prophecy and how Israel is to discern between conflicting prophetic speeches. The lectionary text begins with the description of what a prophet should do

(vv. 15-18) and includes a part of the section dealing with true and false prophecy (vv. 19-20). Whether or not one chooses to expand the boundaries of the lectionary text, interpretation should take place in the larger context of vv. 9-22.

Significance. When preaching this text the congregation should explore what it means to be a prophet. Deuteronomy 18 addresses this question from two points of view, what prophecy should not be (vv. 9-14) and what it should be (vv. 15-18). Preaching Deuteronomy 18 could very well follow the same pattern.

What prophecy is not: Verses 9-14 list a variety of actions that range from the horrifying (child sacrifice in v. 10) to the obscure (divination, soothsaying, auguring, etc. in v. 11). Clearly all of these actions were immediately meaningful for ancient Israel, for they required no detailed description. In preaching this text it would be a mistake to dwell at any length on the details of what these practices may have been, since none of these actions is particularly meaningful today. In addressing what prophecy is not, it is more fruitful to explore what all of these actions have in common. When vv. 9-14 are viewed from this perspective, a unifying theme emerges because each practice is a form of prophecy that seeks to control the future either by prediction or by manipulation of divine power. The writer of Deuteronomy is saying that any attempt to gain security by predicting the future goes against the very nature of the God, because it is a form of manipulation. Such activity, the writer tells us in v. 12 is "abhorrent to the LORD."

The quest to gain access to divine power by predicting the future is just as real in contemporary culture as it was in ancient Israel, even though the acceptable methods of activity have changed. Classic forms of soothsaying still do occur in contemporary life, but they are, for the most part, viewed with suspicion. Recall the problems that Nancy Reagan faced in the 1980s when it was reported that she consulted a psychic to schedule her husband's presidential trips. A much more acceptable form of divination in contemporary culture is the stock market. The entire structure of the stock market is based on divination, because security (now a technical word in economics) ultimately rests in predicting the future earnings of companies. In this larger social context, economists and market analysts are the modern version of ancient soothsayers. Capitalism is a shared belief system in which economists are paid to predict the future outcome of events, precisely because we all have vested interests in knowing how the market will turn. Because it is so powerful in shaping our lives, economics is a form of religion, and when that happens, the prediction of economic outcomes is not just good sound business practice, but it actually becomes divination. It becomes a form of false prophecy that is abhorrent to the Lord, because it competes with the security that only God can offer. If the writer of Deuteronomy were composing today, the seemingly obscure practices of divination in vv. 9-14, would be replaced by much of our everyday economic activity, which would probably be described as the worship of other gods (v. 20).

What prophecy is: A true prophet can only be understood against the backdrop of divination. Three features or criteria of a true prophet are provided in vv. 15-22 in contrast with divination. First, Moses is presented as the ideal of a true prophet. Space does not permit a detailed analysis of the character of Moses in the larger Pentateuch. Yet several features stand out. Moses is reluctant to take on his prophetic duties (the call of Moses). His focus was in bringing a word of God to Israel's present situation, and in modeling that word through example (the deliverance from Egypt and the leading of Israel in the wilderness). Clearly there were future implications to the activity of Moses (the divine promise of land, etc.), yet the power of Moses was not in predicting precise future outcomes (the murmuring traditions that arise because of Moses' inability to predict future outcomes and thus provide the kind of security that Israel desired). Second, the setting from which prophetic leaders must be chosen is the people of God in worship, rather than the larger cultural context. Note how v. 15 specifically limits future prophets to the congregation of Israel. Third, the criteria for evaluating a prophet is past tradition, rather than speculation about the future. This point is made in two ways. (1) Through an appeal to past tradition in vv. 16-18. Moses directs Israel's attention back to Horeb in order to authenticate the office of prophet. Prophets will speak the word of God to Israel because at Mount Horeb, all future revelation was structured through intermediaries. The revelation did not concern speculation about the future, but focused, instead, on the law, which is meant to provide a meaningful system for living the life of faith through time. (2) By rejecting the authority of all divination (future predictions) in vv. 19-22. No prophecy can have authority before it comes true. What appears at first reading to be a caveat to allow for divination—that fulfilled prophecies are true—in fact eliminates all forms of it, because the power of divination is that it must have authority before it comes true. The point of the author seems to be that no divination may have power over us, and, if perchance a future prophecy should come true, then, as fulfilled prophecy it must be viewed as past tradition.

Biblical prophecy is not about the ability to predict events next Tuesday. Rather, it is a form of clairvoyance that arises out of meditation on Scripture. The content of this clairvoyance is insight into the nature of God's security, which then allows us to evaluate critically all forms of false prophecy—forms of divination with conflicting promises of security. The closest analogy to the ideal of true prophecy in Deuteronomy 18 is the preaching of Scripture in the context of worship every Sunday.

The Response: *Psalm 111*

A Hymn of Praise

Setting. Psalm 111 is a hymn of praise in an acrostic form. An acrostic psalm occurs when every line begins with a letter of the Hebrew alphabet, so that by the end of the psalm, the reader has gone through the Hebrew equivalent of the English ABC's.

Structure. Psalm 111 follows the general three-part form of a hymn, which includes an introductory summons to praise, reasons why God should be praised, and a conclusion. The summons to praise occurs in v. 1, where the psalmist declares that God will now be praised in the setting of the worshiping community. The reasons for praise are listed in vv. 2-9, and they focus mostly on God's past acts of salvation. The psalm ends in v. 10 with a didactic conclusion, which encourages other worshipers to be wise by fearing God and by living out this fear.

Significance. When Psalm 111 is read in the context of prophecy, the hymn of praise, itself, takes on a prophetic aspect. This is especially evident in the middle section (vv. 2-9), with the recounting of the past works of God. Deuteronomy 18:16-18 has underscored how knowledge of such past tradition is in fact the basis for prophetic clairvoyance. The correlation between the psalm and Deuteronomy 18 continues into the closing section of the psalm with the motif of fear. The most important result of the revelation on Mount Horeb was that Israel acquired a proper sense of fear (Deuteronomy 5:22-27). This fear of God is what prompted them to choose a prophetic mediator like Moses in the first place, and it is this quality that must provide them with insight in evaluating future prophets. God says as much to Moses in Deuteronomy 5:29: "If only they had such a mind as this, to fear me and to keep all my commandments always, so that it might go well with them and with their children forever!" The motif of fear is not psychological in Deuteronomy, rather it is a form of prophetic clairvoyance. Fear provides insight into the reality of God, which, in turn, establishes the basis for evaluating all other prophetic claims. These qualities of fear reappear in the conclusion to Psalm 111, when the fear of God is linked with ongoing wisdom. The central role of the motif of fear in Psalm 111 suggests that the recital of God's past acts of salvation (vv. 2-9) can be a form of prophecy as well as praise, and that their recitation in worship has the quality of instilling ongoing clairvoyance (wisdom) in the congregation, which, when turned into action, becomes praise to God.

New Testament Texts:

The texts continue the consecutive readings from I Corinthians and Mark. Though there is no overt connection between the passages, in different ways both lessons indicate the limited good of human knowledge, even of human knowledge of divine realities. A topical sermon might work with this theme in relation to both texts, but otherwise the lessons are quite independent of each other.

The Epistle: *I Corinthians 8:1-13*

Love Over Knowledge

Setting. The third major portion of the body of the letter continues, running from the beginning of chapter 8 through chapter 10 (including 11:1). This part of the letter is launched under the rubric of "food sacrificed to idols," but the discussion addresses a variety of topics (e.g., the nature of "knowledge," Christian freedom and responsibility [focusing on the rights of the apostle and Paul's approach to them], the danger of apostasy, and the consumption of idol-meat as food per se). The concern at the heart of Paul's discourse is Christian rights and responsibilities, especially regarding knowledge and freedom.

Structure. There are two distinct sections in the lesson, vv. 1-6 and vv. 7-13, and in the first of these there are three sub-parts, 8:1-3, 4-5, 6. Paul often seems to ramble in these verses and the others, which compose the larger discussion, yet, there is an unfolding logic at work here. In vv. 1-6 Paul repeatedly quotes the Corinthians; then, he responds to them with a counter position, which he explains through theologically based reasoning. The pattern is this: You say/but I say/and here's why. Verses 7-13 continue the rebuttal, but they turn toward strong positive instruction that both exposes the error of the Corinthians' ways and presents a correct Christian life-style. The logic here is this: here's what's wrong/here's what's right. Paul's stark, confrontational style may (or may not) need softening in preaching; the congregational situation will determine that. But his pattern of logic may inspire a dramatic style of rhetorically polished proclamation.

Significance. Verse 1 seems to quote the Corinthians ("all of us possess knowledge") and respond to them ("Knowledge puffs up, but love builds up."). The sharp contrast between knowledge and love exposes the situation in Corinth for what it is—some believers are more interested in acting on their supposedly superior knowledge than in living by the standards of God's love. The problems that result among the Corinthians from this approach show that knowledge is of no certain value in itself. The real criterion of Christian life is not knowledge but love for God, as God loves. To focus on knowledge and to insist upon living in the light of knowledge alone demonstrates genuine lack of Christian comprehension! Paul says what really matters is to be known by God, to be called; and the evidence of Christian calling is love for God, which leads to selfless, not selfish, living.

Because of language and structure, scholars suspect that v. 6 quotes a common early Christian confession which celebrates (literally translated)

1. creation—"There is one God, the Father, out of whom are all things"
2. call—"unto him are we"
3. Christ—"and there is one Lord, Jesus Christ"—
   a. the agent of creation—"through whom are all things"
   b. the agent of redemption—"and through whom are we."

Verses 4-5 show that the Corinthians take this confession and turn it into a speculative thesis that leads to a cocksure attitude and life-style with little concern for others ("Who cares what others think, I know what I am doing!"). Certain sophisticated Corinthians are radically monotheistic so that they confidently deny the reality of idols. Others are less well-informed, and the behavior of the knowledgeable Corinthians scandalizes them. Paul takes the matter and the false gods seriously! Love, not knowledge, motivates and directs correct Christian living—with others ahead of self.

In vv. 7-13 Paul turns up the heat. He corrects "the strong" and tells them how they are to relate to "the weak." The strong are told that it is not a matter of the holiness or unholiness of a substance that matters; rather, what counts is loving conduct in relation to fellow believers. Christians are not merely liberated to do their own thing, they are free in the context of the new creation for concerned living in relation to others. Freedom is not a personal abstract right, it is a concrete Christian reality shown appropriately in concern. Real freedom is being freed from the necessity to assert only, or primarily, one's own rights! Verse 11 states the strange, sad irony of loveless knowledge directing daily living: "By your knowledge those weak believers for whom Christ died are destroyed." Paul's point is transparent. This world's contention that "it's okay to do as you please as long as you know what you're doing, no matter what others think" is the self-centered, destructive disposition of a Christless culture. Knowledge has the potential to destroy as well as to liberate. Thus knowledge must be subordinated to love.

The Gospel: *Mark 1:21-28*

Jesus' Power as a Teacher

Setting. Mark 1:21-39 is a section of the Gospel recounting four stories about occurrences on the first Sabbath and the following morning of Jesus' ministry. A temporal and geographical specificity to this material suggests that Mark coordinated these stories deliberately into a large complex unit. Our lesson is the first of the four stories, focusing on an exorcism and results.

Structure. The story is set in a synagogue in Capernaum on a Sabbath. First-century readers would assume an "atmosphere" where a community of faith was gathered for scripture reading, commentary, and instruction in relation to the scripture, and (in general) worship. Even informal synagogue worship had purpose and order. That order is disrupted, however, by the chaos caused by the demoniac. Jesus confronts the disruptive force, demonstrating superior power. This show of authority produces amazement, wonder in awe, which issues in affirmation of Jesus' teaching. Themes such as pious order, chaos, confrontation, divine power, restoration of order, confirmation, amazement, affirmation, and teaching in power are possible subjects for proclamation.

Significance. Anyone coming to this passage in the twentieth century faces immediate difficulties. The difference between first- and twentieth-century sensibilities concerning demons, exorcisms, and the miraculous are great. An ancient with a headache blamed a demon and prayed, whereas even the most pious, conservative, Bible-believing citizen of the twentieth century (perhaps with the exception of the charismatic Christian in so-called spiritual warfare) who suffers such pain is more likely to blame food, atmosphere, sinuses, or stress and to take an aspirin than to think of the demonic and the divine.

Past generations of scholars have struggled to understand and explain biblical miracle stories, even to the point of explaining the miracles away through rationalistic or psychological explanations (most of which are anachronistic and sheerly speculative). While today we are more aware of and sometimes more honest about the limits of our knowledge, it is not fully necessary to rehabilitate demons in order to use texts such as this one for valid biblical preaching. Even in the context of the first-century Church this text was a vehicle for communicating a message larger than the claim that Jesus did an exorcism. This miracle story declares Jesus' true identity, demonstrates his divine authority, and defines his teaching with power.

This story tells us that the same power that enabled Jesus to compel the demonic forces to obey him was at work in his teaching. In both vv. 22 and 27 Mark underscores the amazement of the people at the teaching Jesus did. No mean pedagogue, he taught with an authority the crowds had not seen. The statement of the crowd after Jesus' exorcism of the demon is a very odd remark, "What is this? A new teaching—with authority!" Its oddity drives home Mark's central point. Jesus taught with uncommon authority. His words and his ways were above the common run of human instruction. There was a clear continuity, coherence, and consistency between what Jesus said and what he did that validated his ministry of word and deed. By way of illustration, one of the most effective public speakers of the twentieth century was asked to explain his success. "It's simple," he said, "know what you think and why, and mean every word you say."

The story also teaches about the identity of Jesus. The demoniac recognizes him—"I know who you are, the Holy One of God." The validity of this identification comes in the power displayed in the exorcism. Here we see God's power at work in the world. Jesus Christ liberates a human from bondage to the demonic force(s) that had reduced life to a sub-human level beneath the actual will of God.

Though the outcome of Jesus' ministry is amazement that motivates the spreading abroad of his fame, the achievement of fame is not Jesus' goal. He commands the demoniac to silence, so that it is despite his actions as well as because of them that he achieves notoriety. Mark's story carries the subtle but profound message that knowing about Jesus is not the same thing as experiencing his liberating power. Jesus' teaching becomes effective in the transformation of human life, not merely in being repeated and discussed.

EPIPHANY 4: THE CELEBRATION

All three lessons today help provide a basis for a sermonic discussion of the meaning and purpose of preaching in the Christian Church. The Old Testament lesson is concerned with what true prophecy is all about. The epistle lesson begins by emphasizing that Christian witness involves more than "inside knowledge." The Gospel lesson portrays Christ as a preacher whose authority is obvious because of "a clear continuity, coherence, and consistency between what Jesus said and what he did" (see comment above).

Given that congregations spend so much time listening to sermons, it is always amazing to discover how little they think about the process. While there is no doubt that sermon evaluation does go on informally, church members often shrink from being involved in more structured critique sessions, because, they say, they don't know enough. A kind of gnostic mystique about preaching is implied here. They may be quick to add that "they know what they like." What they need help with is relating "what they like" to the Church's ministry of preaching. For that reason a sermon about the congregation's involvement in the homiletical process may be in order today.

On the basis of the Old Testament lesson, one might speak of prophetic preaching as an event based in the tradition of helping the assembly remember, in the anamestic sense of making present, God's saving activity through the ages. How does preaching help the congregation recall, re-experience, and recite the old, old story? The epistle lesson provides the critique of love to preaching as a remedy against the "trendies" of whatever stripe who wish to reduce the gospel to an unquestioning allegiance to any one party or point of view. An active listener should always be asking, "What corner is the preacher backing me into here?" And the Gospel lesson makes clear the Christocentric character of the Church's proclamation. By this is not meant signing a doctrinal confession or a statement affirming creedal purity. Rather, it has to do with the overcoming of the demons by the power of love and the liberating of those enslaved to forces of degradation. Does the Church's preaching help persons realize that a freedom is being offered them, which they do not deserve and which they cannot earn? The preacher may wish to help the congregation explore the issue of authority in preaching: where does it come from and how is it recognized?

A hymn by Thomas Troeger and Carol Doran, "Silence! Frenzied, Unclean Spirit," is based on today's Gospel lesson. It can be found in their book *New Hymns for the Lectionary* (New York: Oxford University Press, 1986) and is reprinted in *The United Methodist Hymnal*. Most of the hymns in *New Hymns for the Lectionary* are based on an older edition of the B-cycle, and so can be an on-going resource for worship planning during this year.

Fifth Sunday After Epiphany

Old Testament Texts

Isaiah 40:21-31, which celebrates God's incomparable power, is a message of salvation at a time of hopelessness for Israel. Psalm 147:1-11, 20*c* is a song of praise that is based in God's domination over creation.

The Lesson: *Isaiah 40:21-31*

You Can't Always Believe in What You Feel

Setting. The commentary for the call of Second Isaiah in Isaiah 40:1-11 from the Second Sunday of Advent also serves as the central commentary for Isaiah 40:21-31. What follows is specific analysis of the form and structure of Isaiah 40:12-31.

Isaiah 40:21-31 consists of a series of disputations about whether God was able to bring about a new salvation even in the worst possible circumstances—the Exile. The central argument at the core of these disputations is the quotation of Israel in v. 27, "My way is hidden from the LORD, and my right is disregarded by my God." This quotation may very well be part of a lamentation that was used in Israel's worship during the exilic period. Although the quotation has a pious ring to it, it masks a small faith that could not conceive of God acting in the world beyond the boundaries of the community's experience. The disputation is about the shortsightedness of such a belief.

Structure. The lectionary reading is part of a larger section that includes vv. 12-31. This section consists of four disputation speeches: vv. 12-17 argue for the incomprehensibility of God; vv. 18-24 and 25-26 argue for the incomparability of God, and vv. 27-31 argue for God's ability to save Israel even during the Exile. Note how the first three disputations really presuppose the last one, because it is only in v. 27 that we learn of Israel's lament. The rhetorical questions in the first disputation (Who has measured? directed? taught? vv. 12, 13, 14), which then continue in the second and third speeches where the emphasis shifts to comparison ("To whom then will you liken God?" vv. 18, 25) are all meant to address Israel's lament in v. 27. The last disputation is more complete than the previous three because it includes this lament. This development has prompted scholars to suggest that the first three disputations are meant to function as an introduction for the final one. In any case this development underscores how the lectionary text lacks clear boundaries by beginning at v. 21 and should probably be extended back to at least v. 18 where the second disputation begins.

Significance. The lament in v. 27 is the key for preaching Isaiah 40. How do we maintian hope in God's ability to save when such a confession contradicts all aspects of our experience? Second Isaiah's answer is that God the creator is more than the sum total of our experience. The creator is incomprehensible and incomparable to anything that we can imagine. Therefore it is impossible to say at any time and under any circumstances that our way is hidden from God, or that God might become indifferent to our situation in life even when events would suggest otherwise. Such a confession is radical because it critically evaluates all experience. The Christian faith is rooted in such a radical confession. Nothing in our life experience leads to the conclusion of a resurrection. Yet the belief that we die and then are recreated in a new world goes to the heart of Christianity. Such a belief critically evaluates all aspects of our experience because it is ultimately rooted in the same creative power of God for which Second Isaiah passionately argues in vv. 12-31.

The Response: *Psalm 147:1-11, 20c*

A Song of Praise

Setting. Psalm 147 is a song of praise. It begins with an imperative in v. 1, "Praise the Lord" (Hallelujah!), which is followed by two reasons for praising God: because it is good to sing praises to God and because it is pleasant. The remainder of the psalm provides illustrations of God's character that are meant to fill out the opening imperative.

Structure. Psalm 147 separates into three parts: vv. 1-6, 7-11, 12-20. The lectionary reading includes vv. 1-11 and the final verse. Each of the two sections in vv. 1-11 are clearly separated by imperatives, calling for praise to God (v. 1 begins with "Praise the Lord," and v. 7, "Sing to the Lord").

Significance. The most striking feature of Psalm 147:1-11, 20 is the way in which the psalm moves back and forth between the creative and salvific power of God, between the vastness of cosmology and concrete deeds of salvation. These two different kinds of divine action and power merge into one song of praise. The first stanza illustrates this point in vv. 2-6. After the opening call to praise in v. 1, concrete images of salvation are sketched out in vv. 2-3 and 6. Verses 2-3 recount the return from exile—Jerusalem is rebuilt and the exiles return, while v. 6 generalizes from this experience in order to outline a reversal that is characteristic of God's salvation—wicked are brought low and downtrodden are lifted up. Between these images of salvation, vv. 4-5 describe the power of God in the outer reaches of the cosmos. The central motif in this section is the word *number*. It begins v. 4 ("the number of the stars") and it ends v. 5 ("his understanding is beyond measure" [the Hebrew word used means "number"]). The framing of these verses with the word *number* emphasizes the "otherness" of God and his incomprehensible character. The juxtaposition of the incomprehensible power of God in the cosmos (vv. 4-5) and concrete instances of this power in the life of the people of God (vv. 2-3, 6) gives the song of praise both vastness and intimacy at the same time.

The second stanza continues to review the creative power of God in the life of the people of God (vv. 8-9), before drawing some conclusions about how humans should live. The conclusion of the second section is that even though God is powerful, he does not particularly enjoy it in creatures or in humans (v. 10). Rather what God enjoys are those who trust in his power (v. 11).

New Testament Texts

The lessons continue the sequential readings from I Corinthians and Mark. Inherent in both lessons are profound statements, quite different but genuinely complementary, about the self-giving nature of Christian living.

The Epistle: *I Corinthians 9:16-23*

The Freedom to Exercise Rights Responsibly

Setting. Having discussed Christian freedom and responsibility in relation to the "strong" and the "weak" and their relationship to one another in chapter 8, I Corinthians 9 is a three-part excursus on the rights of an apostle. In the first part of the excursus (9:1-18) Paul describes these apostolic rights, gives their logical and scriptural bases, and explains why he foregoes such rights. This leads to the second part of his reflections (9:19-23), which treats Paul's style of ministry and its motivations. The third element in the excursus (9:24-27) discusses the need for discipline in ministry—and, by implication, in Christian life—its goal, and its extent.

Structure. Our lesson comprises the last verses of the first part of the excursus and the entire second section of it. Verses 15-18 cohere, explaining why Paul does not take support from the congregation, because he understands himself to be compelled to do ministry. Then, vv. 19-23 elaborate the idea of Paul's apostolic freedom, which means total selflessness. Four basic ideas are unfolded: necessity, generosity, freedom, and selflessness. The logic is progressive and cumulative, and Paul's statements are concrete, not abstract.

Significance. Paul declares that he is an apostle because he was conscripted into God's service. He did not enlist in the ranks of the apostles, rather God commissioned Paul. Paul is no mercenary. If Paul preaches because God commands it, his doing so is no credit to him—it is but obedience. Paul sees no merit in mere compliance with God's will, though he understands he would be in dire circumstances if he were disobedient. Yet Paul is crafty. He has found a way to earn a reward even while merely being obedient. As an apostle he has rights to basic support from those to whom he preaches and among whom he works, but he chooses to forego this support. By doing so he gives up what is rightfully his, making of it an offering to God. Strikingly, Paul's "reward" is that he takes no reward from his work. *The joy of giving service free of charge is Paul's reward.*

Moreover, as a Christian apostle, Paul is truly free. Because he comprehends the radical nature of Christian freedom, Paul could be at liberty to live in whatever manner he elects—for, as the Corinthians say, all things are permissible! (see 6:12). Yet, Paul chooses to relinquish his personal freedom in order to be as effective as possible in service. He will allow nothing to come between his message and those to whom he preaches. If issues of life-style are barriers or hang-ups, Paul simply sets his rightful freedom from Christ aside and takes on the burden of others' (obviously weaker) consciences. Paul varies his personal behavior in order to win both Jews and those outside the law.

Verse 23 is crucial. Paul says, "I do all this because of the gospel, in order that I may become its partner." In other words, the gospel presides over Paul as a kind of senior partner. In working as a junior partner to the gospel, Paul ministers in such a way that the gospel is not relativized to worldly social conditions (i.e., contemporary social structures and sensibilities), rather he is!

Paul's remarks in the verses of this lesson take us far from the frequent misperception of Paul as a rigid, inflexible, arrogant man. As we listen we hear him discussing how he makes himself a tool of the gospel for the sake of the salvation of others, even though this means he loses his God-given rights as he caters to the sensitivities of others. As is clear from Paul's letters in general, the apostle was no chameleon; yet, we learn that his own rights are less important than the integrity of the gospel and the capacity of others to hear the gospel without unnecessary hang-ups.

In the Church today we are frequently so intent upon claiming our rights that we attempt to force-feed our life-styles to those who have other sensibilities. We have yet to learn that there are legitimate ambiguities in Christian living and that we may indeed have quite different but equally valid claims on a Christian pattern of behavior. We have too little of Paul's flexibility and personal modesty. How many of us actually put both the gospel and the sensitivities of others ahead of ourselves? When we adopt the position that the gospel means something for me and mine before it means something for you and yours, then we have abdicated Christlike living.

The Gospel: *Mark 1:29-39*

The Nature of Ministry, the Character of Christ, and the Primacy of Preaching

Setting. This lesson continues in the section begun with last week's Gospel reading. Readers are asked to consult that earlier discussion of the setting of the Gospel text for additional information. Here it is sufficient to recall that Mark's placement and sequencing of the materials from 1:21-39 suggests he intended to present the stories in this section as a block of related materials.

Structure. Verses 29-39 present three distinct incidents. First, vv. 29-31 recount the healing of Simon's mother-in-law; second, vv. 32-34 tell of healings and exorcisms Jesus did at evening time; and, third, vv. 35-39 recall Jesus' going out for private prayer and the subsequent beginning of his preaching tour. In turn, we learn that Jesus cures those in need of healing; Jesus cares for those who come to him; and Jesus declares the priority of preaching!

Significance. Readers may wish to consult the discussion of the difficulty of preaching in relation to miracle stories in the section on "significance" for last week's Gospel lesson, since the first two sections of our reading continue to deal with healings and exorcisms.

The story of Jesus' healing of Simon's mother-in-law is inherently profound, though it is easy to miss the significance of this text. First, the sickness, described as fever, would immediately be understood by ancients to have a demonic cause. Thus, Jesus' act of healing is active defeat of the forces of evil, as was the case with the previous overt exorcism. Mark shows us Jesus doing God's work in the world in order to defeat evil and to reestablish God's own will in relation to human life. Health not sickness is God's desire, and in Jesus we see God's power at work to achieve wholeness for humans in need of health. Second, the manner in which Mark describes the healed woman's activities after she is restored is striking. We are told literally that "she ministered to them." The verb used here is one which Mark employs in a restricted and seemingly deliberate way. Jesus declares that he came "to minister" (10:45); we read that angels "ministered" to Jesus (1:13); and Mark tells us that, here, Simon's mother-in-law "ministered to them," and, later, that the Galilean women who followed Jesus and saw his crucifixion "ministered to him" (15:41). The angels and Jesus are clearly under God's authority or, at least, they are the ones who are doing God's will in Mark's story. But what about the women? Perhaps the most helpful interpretive clue is found in Mark 10:45, where Jesus himself says, "The Son of Man came not to be served but to serve, and to give his life a ransom for many." The issue in service is total vulnerability. Because of their social position in Jewish culture, women were generally vulnerable, not powerful; yet Mark may be telling us that those who are truly vulnerable are capable of true service, or ministry, because they are freed by their lack of power to be genuinely selfless. This understanding does not romanticize powerlessness or oppression, but it prefers strength in weakness and godliness in concern with others over self.

The second story in this group of three is essentially christological in nature. Jesus is shown to be the source of God's healing, redemptive power. Jesus is able and does restore those who come to him for assistance. In this story the line between healing and exorcism is very fine, for ancients generally assumed that illness was the result of some form of demonic oppression. Thus we see Jesus doing battle with the forces of evil and triumphing over whatever stands in opposition to God's will. Indeed, this "message" is emphasized by the information that the demons recognized Jesus and he commanded them to silence. This brief account makes clear God's will, God's power, God's purposes, and the identity and relationship of Jesus to each and all of these items.

Finally, we have a story that underscores the importance of preaching in the ministry of Jesus. As the story in last week's lesson (Mark 1:21-28) pointed to the power inherent in Jesus' teaching, in turn, this story shows us that the work of Jesus is not exhausted in the doing of physical miracles. There are forms of oppression other than physical ailment, and the power of God comes in the person and work of Jesus Christ in order to liberate persons in need of hearing the good news of God's love. Preaching itself is presented as an act of the saving power of God. If Jesus would not allow himself to become completely mired in acts of physical kindness, but insisted through the insight of prayer that proclamation was as necessary or even more necessary than doing good works, then we should heed his example and give of our time and efforts to proclamation, or at least in this world to gossiping the gospel. None of us will ever simply do or be good enough to ensure that the will of God is made plain in this world. We are called to speak as Christ himself necessarily spoke. Today the preaching of the gospel has acquired a bad image because of the actions of charlatans, but their hypocrisy does not undo our commission to declare the great goodness of God's love in Jesus Christ.

EPIPHANY 5: THE CELEBRATION

Today's Old Testament lesson suggests as a bulletin cover a reproduction of the etching by William Blake that portrays God as the Great Artificer leaning over the globe and firmament with a compass. Around the drawing could be inscribed from the lesson "It is he who sits above the circle of the earth" (Isaiah 40:22a).

The following adaptation of Isaiah 40:27-31 from the scriptural paraphrases of the Church of Scotland may be used as an opening hymn. St. Peter fits well for four-line stanzas. For eight-line stanzas Materna (O beautiful for spacious skies) perhaps matches best the mood of the lines.

> Why pourest forth thine anxious cry,
> despairing of relief,

As if the Lord o'erlooked thy cause,
    and did not heed thy grief?

Hast thou not known, hast thou not heard,
    that firm remains on high
The everlasting throne of him
    who formed the earth and sky?

Art thou afraid his power shall fail
    when comes thy evil day?
And can an all-creating arm
    grow weary and decay?

Supreme in wisdom as in power
    the Rock of ages stands;
Though him thou canst not see, nor trace
    the working of his hands.

He gives the conquest to the weak,
    supports the fainting heart;
And courage in the evil hour
    his heavenly aids impart.

Mere human power shall fast decay,
    and youthful vigor cease;
But they who wait upon the Lord
    in strength shall still increase.

They with unwearied feet shall tread
    the path of life divine;
With growing ardor onward move,
    with growing brightness shine.

On eagles' wings they mount, they soar,
    their wings are faith and love,
'Til, past the cloudy regions here,
    they rise to heaven above.

The epistle and Gospel lessons suggest that the theme of preaching and its meaning might be continued for today's sermon. The centrality of private prayer in the life of Jesus is particularly remarkable in the pericope. It points to the source of power for all of Jesus' ministry. Preaching cannot be divorced from the preacher, so it is not inappropriate for the preacher to talk with the congregation about her/his identification with the task, even as Paul does to the congregation at Corinth.

Paul's example must be fully followed, however, so that the sermon is not a self-serving exercise, but directs the hearers' attention to the apostolic rather than the individual commission. "Apostolic succession" in the Protestant sense involves an ongoing struggle with the scriptural text that reflects the world of the apostles. As Adolf Schlatter put it:

> The chief thing in the service of worship is not your opinion, as you may be inclined to present it in your sermon; the chief thing is and remains the text. Guilt is not absolved and the dying are not raised up by your believing and opining; here it must be: Thus it is written; this is what the messenger of Jesus is saying to you. For the ministry, therefore, the first and most important duty is to keep open the lines of communication and community with the apostles, in order that we may use their message at the right time and in the right way. To use it we must know it and to know it we must remain in communication with them. (Quoted in John W. Doberstein, ed., *Minister's Prayer Book* [Philadelphia: Muhlenberg Press, n.d.], p. 409)

Today's Gospel lesson may also provide an opportunity to discuss with the worship committee, if not in the sermon itself, the place of anointing and prayers for healing in the congregation's life. To what degree should these be public, to what degree private occasions?

It is unfortunate that the abandoning of evening services in many churches has meant the loss of many beautiful hymns. One of the most beautiful, "At Even, ere the Sun Was Set," was based on today's lesson from Mark. It can be found in most older hymnals and might be resurrected for this day, since both text and tune are in the public domain. The first line of the second stanza, with its reference to it being evening, may be amended to "As such they were, so even we." And in the last stanza "evening hour" can be changed to "worship hour."

Sixth Sunday After Epiphany

Old Testament Texts

Second Kings 5:1-14 is the story of how Elisha cured the leprosy of Naaman. Psalm 30 is the thanksgiving of a sick person who has recovered.

The Lesson: *II Kings 5:1-14*

The Healing of Naaman

Setting. The healing of Naaman is one episode in the larger cycle of stories about Elisha, the prophet. Elisha is introduced in I Kings 19 as the successor of Elijah and becomes the central figure in a series of stories in II Kings 2–9, before his death is recorded in II Kings 13. Many miracle stories circulate around the character of Elisha. He purifies food and water, miraculously feeds one hundred people, raises children from the dead, and is able to cure disease. Even after his death, contact with his bones prompts a resurrection. The story of Naaman's cure from leprosy fits into this larger cycle of miracle stories.

Structure. The boundaries of the lectionary text are limited to the healing of Naaman. His story actually continues through v. 19 where his return to the prophet and conversion to Yahwism is narrated. Then a story of the swindling of Naaman by Elisha's servant, Gehazi, rounds out the chapter. The lectionary text can be separated into four parts. The problem of the narrative is established in vv. 1-3: Naaman has leprosy. The next two sections, vv. 4-7 and 8-12 narrate two intermediate and unsuccessful attempts by Naaman to resolve his problem, until he is finally cured by Elisha in vv. 13-14.

Significance. Many of the commentaries approach this story around its central dynamic of a problem (leprosy in Naaman) seeking a solution (healing from leprosy). And, indeed, this structure is essential for interpreting the story. There is a certain balance in the telling of the story between characters as the plot unravels toward its solution. In the opening section (vv. 1-3) Naaman is introduced, his problem is stated and a servant girl suggests a solution by mentioning the prophet in Samaria (Elisha) who is able to work miracles. Somewhat surprisingly the King of Aram supports Naaman's trip to Israel and sends a letter of introduction with his commander. The king of Israel presents the first obstacle to this solution in the second section (vv. 4-7) by interpreting Naaman's quest for a cure (and the king's letter) as a political ruse to engage Israel in battle. Naaman, himself, presents the second obstacle in the third section (vv. 8-12). He is a person of high rank who is accustomed to special treatment. And when the prophet does not even bother to leave his tent to give directions on how he might cure himself (washing in the Jordan River seven times), Naaman is offended. He is rescued from his arrogance by his servants in vv. 13-14 (a parallel to the servant girl in the opening section) and thus is healed. This synopsis underscores how there is art in the telling of the story, but such literary insight still leaves open the question of how to preach this text.

The cure of Naaman is a story about the activity of God beyond the boundaries of Israel. The problem in the story, therefore, is how people go about recognizing the activity of God in unexpected places. This point is carried through the story by keeping the activity of God in the background. There is no divine revelation or prophetic speech in the narrative. Instead the actions of characters determine the degree to which God enters the story. The Israelite king and Naaman represent the two major obstacles. The most negative character in the story is the king, who cannot conceive of God being active beyond the boundaries of Israel. A request for a miracle from Israel's God, therefore, could not possibly be sincere, and it is interpreted as a ruse for battle. Naaman is a mixed character. Verse 1 introduces the tension that surrounds him. He has leprosy and he has found favor with the Lord. Three questions arise. First, why the combination of leprosy and divine favor, since leprosy frequently functions as a sign of divine judgment, as it does at the close of the story with Gehazi? And second, why does God like Naaman at all? He is not an Israelite. And finally, will Naaman be able to recognize this divine favor?

God lurks in the background, thus leaving all of these questions open. Elisha functions almost as indirectly as God in this story, and, in fact, as the healer he comes to embody divine power in the story. Thus, even though this is an episode in the larger cycle of Elisha stories, the prophet does not take center stage. Instead, it is a story about Naaman, but the real heroes who bring about the transformation of Naaman are the minor characters that surround him—the Israelite servant girl and his servants who accompany him to the prophet. The result of their actions is his cure and conversion. In the end there appear to be two points, which are related in a paradoxical way, in preaching this story. First, God is indeed active independently beyond the boundaries of the people of God—for whatever reason Naaman found favor with God. And, second, the only way that God's independent activity can come into clear focus is through the people of God—the servant girl and Elisha.

The Response: *Psalm 30*

A Hymn of Thanksgiving

Setting. Psalm 30 is a hymn of thanksgiving over having been healed. Verse 2 reads: "O Lord my God, I cried to you for help, and you have healed me."

Structure. Psalm 30 separates into three parts. It begins in vv. 1-3 with praise to God for rescuing the psalmist. Verses 4-5 shift the focus from God to fellow worshipers when the psalmist calls for those around him to join in giving thanksgiving to God. In vv. 6-12 the psalmist recounts his life changes and how God rescued him. This section closes with a summary statement outlining the purpose of divine deliverance: It is so that the psalmist can continue to praise God.

Significance. The account of divine healing is meant to emphasize a change of direction that was experienced by the psalmist. He recounts his movement from prosperity (v. 6) to near death (v. 9) and back again to the world of the living (v. 11). The movement provides direct commentary on Naaman.

New Testament Texts

Though the lessons essentially are the results of the sequential readings of I Corinthians and Mark, they teach important theological lessons that complement each other. Paul is concerned with the basic shape of Christian life, the necessity of discipline, and the determinative work of the Holy Spirit; whereas Mark's story reveals important truths about the will of God in relation to humanity which, in turn, motivates one toward the disciplined life to which Paul calls.

The Epistle: *I Corinthians 9:24-27*

Training for Christian Living

Setting. As we saw in considering the reading for the Fifth Sunday After Epiphany, in I Corinthians 9 Paul offers a three-part excursus on the rights of an apostle. The reading for this week is the third portion of Paul's remarks (9:24-27) wherein he discusses the need for discipline in ministry—and, by implication, in Christian life—its goal and its extent. Paul builds here on the foregoing comments in the larger excursus, so that it may be helpful to re-read vv. 1-23 as they lead into the four verses of our present text.

Structure. In these verses Paul employs a collection of images from athletic endeavors to teach the Corinthians. The organization of the unit seems to spiral in its logic, moving around and forward by going from image to explanation over and over. There is logical progress in Paul's thought, however, and this is suggestive for the structure of sermons. Describing the verses somewhat abstractly, one finds Paul considering (1) how Christians press for a prize, (2) the necessity of self-control, (3) the necessity of direction in life, and (4) the crucial nature of disciplined discipleship.

Significance. Paul takes up a striking, stimulating set of athletic images employing them metaphorically to explain and advocate a disciplined life for the members of the congregation in Corinth. This manner of teaching would have been especially meaningful for the Corinthians because every two years in the spring Corinth was the sight of the Isthmian games, a far-ranging athletic competition which ranked only below the Olympic Games in prestige. In v. 24 Paul speaks of the runners. They run for a prize; yet Paul reminds the Corinthians that only one runner succeeds. Likewise, Paul says Christians are out to pursue a prize. The metaphor is inexact and should not be pressed, for a sheer exclusiveness that would promote competitiveness is not Paul's point; rather, he admonished the members of the Corinthian church to an active life-style. What is the prize? Paul does not say explicitly, but the mention of the "imperishable" wreath in v. 25 suggests "salvation," as in "resurrection," would be a reasonable understanding.

In v. 25 Paul moves on to refer to "self-control in all things." As possessors of a larger collection of Paul's epistles (unlike the Corinthians) we may immediately think of Paul's well-known words in Galatians 5:22-23, "By contrast, the fruit of the Spirit is love, joy, peace, patience, kindness, generosity, faithfulness, gentleness, and self-control. There is no law against such things." This illuminating parallel passage makes clear two important items. First, the self-control that Paul advocates is not merely a human work. He is not simply saying, "Be good!" Rather, such self-control exists in the lives of believers because of the indwelling work of the Holy Spirit. Second, this is a universal gift of the Spirit, and it is to be expected in every Christian life; it is not a special gift available to but a few who are to employ it in service to the many. Self-control characterizes all real Christian living—a lesson the Corinthians need badly to take to heart. In relation to this element in Paul's words to the Corinthians each preacher will have to determine whether and how her or his congregation needs to hear this same message.

Verse 26 extends Paul's metaphor. He says he does not run "aimlessly"—that is, without direction or goal. From this point, Paul leaps to the image of boxing. Now, he declares that he does not "box as though beating the air"—literally, "not fanning the air"—in the style of an untrained boxer. It is not that Paul is boxing nothing, rather his image is that of an expert pugilist whose punches count because they hit their mark. Thus, in both images—runner and boxer—Paul declares that his efforts are focused; readers should understand the focus comes from discipline.

Verse 27 is almost shocking, for Paul reveals that his opponent is himself. Surely this is a lesson for the Corinthians whose attitude had led to the kind of easy, self-indulgent living that merely presumes upon God's grace and does not relate in obedience to God's saving acts. Paul's shocking revelation declares literally that he "blackens the eye of his body and subjugates it" lest he be disqualified himself through inappropriate lenience. Having called for discipline, the apostle also warns against the very real possibility of substandard performance! In context, this is more a call to dependence on the working of the Holy Spirit in our lives than an exhortation to achievement.

The Gospel: *Mark 1:40-45*

Seeing Humanity Through Jesus' Eyes

Setting. This week's Gospel lesson is again located in the section begun with the Gospel reading of two weeks ago. Readers are asked to consult the discussion of the setting of the Gospel text for the previous two weeks for additional information. Following the complex of stories given in the lesson for last week, we now encounter a seemingly independent story about the healing of a leper, which concludes with a report about Jesus' increasing fame and his subsequent retreat to the country. Scholars find no specific "historical" reason for Mark's having located these verses in their current context, but many commentators judge that this material is placed here for literary and theological reasons, above all, these verses serve to clarify the character of Jesus' work.

Structure. The story is formed around the simple framework of an ancient miracle story in three parts: description of the sickness or problem, action taken for mitigation of the difficulty, and a statement and/or an action in confirmation of the "miracle." In its brevity the story is typical of such ancient accounts, yet despite its terseness, there are both remarkable elements within the basic story and an appendage concerning the healed man's report about Jesus and the necessity of Jesus' move into the countryside.

Significance. The sociology of ancient Israel (and other portions of the Mediterranean world) helps us in an initial effort to understand this account. Behind this story lies a major concern of ancients, the issue of what is clean and what is unclean and, in turn, the separation of the two. Standards for determining what was clean and unclean occupied many ancient cultures, including Israel. At root this was a religious matter; for through the distinguishing of what was clean from what was unclean, ancients made religious statements about what was "in" and what was "out" in relation to the favor of the divine. The leper in this story was "out." His very illness was taken to be the clearest possible evidence that God did not care for him, indeed in divine anger God visited this blight upon him; thus he was designated "unclean" and relegated to the fringes of normal society, outcast by others because he was believed to be cast out by God.

Remarkably, this man approached Jesus. How he knew of him and why he would dare come to him requesting healing we cannot say, but quite clearly the man has not accepted the judgment of society that his illness is God's doing as a sign of displeasure. The man's coming is itself a judgment on the heartless character of religion that fails to grasp the essential truth of divine compassion and that perpetuates the cruelest lie that God is a demanding despot rather than the God of love. Despite his sickness and social rejection, though perhaps because of and through it, the man had come to see that should Jesus desire to do so, he can make him clean. The man's request calls for the revelation of the truth about God.

This reading of the story finds confirmation in the way that Mark tells of the words, actions, and even emotions of Jesus in response to this man's request. As Mark reports the events, we find a strange cluster of reactions and statements attributed to Jesus. At first when he regards the man, Jesus is filled with compassion, so that he declares his willingness to heal him and even goes so far as to touch him, an act which normally would have rendered Jesus himself unclean. As it turns out, however, we find that Jesus has the greater power; for he is not made unclean, but the man is made whole, clean! Thus we see the will and the power of God at work in the words and works of Jesus.

Yet, implicit in the narration of this story is the "historical" and "theological" memory of Jesus' critique of exclusive, rigid religion. In Mark's narration in Greek (v. 43) we catch a glimpse of Jesus' anger in this situation. The language behind "after sternly warning him" more literally suggests anger; but why? and toward whom or what? Surely not the man, although the charge to silence (which is immediately disobeyed because some things are too good to keep to yourself!), which is part of the well-known "Messianic Secret" in Mark, might mislead one into that notion. Yet look at the following words! The man is commanded to perform the letter of the law in order to demonstrate not only that he is clean, but as a proof of God's love to "them"—that is, those people who would rather see God as anger than God as love.

The final note about the man's talking and Jesus' fame moves the basic story forward. But this note may be helpful for preaching since it recalls the results of Jesus' actions, which may guide the purposes and goals of the sermon.

EPIPHANY 6: THE CELEBRATION

The lesson of Naaman washing in the Jordan and being made clean provides a scriptural warrant for the administration of baptism on this day for those churches that are concerned with having sacramental actions reflect some aspect of the biblical narrative. Washing from sin is not the only image appropriate for baptism, but it is the emphasis that can be made from today's texts about both Naaman and the leper in the Gospel lesson.

The following prayer, adapted from Psalm 51 with its reference to washing, may serve as the Confession of Sin in this service:

Have mercy upon us, O God,
according to your loving kindness.
According to the multitude of your tender mercies
blot out our transgressions.
Wash us thoroughly from our iniquities,
and cleanse us from our sins.
We acknowledge our transgressions,
and our sin is ever before us.
Create in us clean hearts, O God,
and renew a right spirit within us;
through Jesus Christ our Lord. Amen.

Following the prayer there may be time for private recollection and confession, and then the following Wesley stanzas may be sung prior to the minister's declaration of pardon:

Now, Lord, to whom for help I call,
Thy miracles repeat;
With pitying eyes behold me fall
A leper at thy feet.

From sin, the guilt, the power, the pain,
Thou wilt redeem my soul;
Lord, I believe, and not in vain—
That faith shall make me whole.
[1780 Collection, 131:3; 132:10, altered]

A meditative tune such as St. Agnes is suggested.

The story of Naaman raises the issue of what has been called the scandal of particularity, the fact that God appears to choose particular means as a source of revelation and saving activity. Naaman echoes our rational objections: Why wash in the Jordan? Why aren't the rivers back home good enough? If God can perform this miracle in the first place, then why be picky about the details? The answer must involve one's theology of the Incarnation, the fact that God gets particular enough to dwell in a particular human body at a particular time in history. This becomes the basis for our sacramental activity, and so baptisms on this day can be illustrative of this character of God. The point is not that God is limited to working in these precise ways but that God can be depended upon to work in and through them.

The epistle lesson allows for the third in a series of sermons on the place of preaching in the Church. The theme today concerns the self-discipline that is necessary for both clergy and laity if they are to witness effectively about the freedom to be found in Christ. Paul's image of the athlete is one of freedom that can only be realized by acknowledging one's limits and practicing self-control. The hymn, "Make Me a Captive, Lord," captures the essence of Paul's thought for today.

Seventh Sunday After Epiphany

Old Testament Texts

Isaiah 43:18-25 includes sections of an oracle of salvation and a trial speech. Psalm 41 is the song of thanksgiving.

The Lesson: *Isaiah 43:18-25*

Salvation and a Defense of Judgment

Setting. A form-critical analysis of the lectionary text makes it clear that the present boundaries cut across two distinct units. Isaiah 43:16-21 is an oracle of salvation and Isaiah 43:22-28 is a disputation between God and Israel staged as a trial.

Structure. The form-critical analysis leads to two separate outlines. The expected structure of an oracle of salvation includes (1) a community lament, (2) a proclamation of salvation, and (3) a glimpse of the end result of God's salvation. Isaiah 43:16-21 has departed from this form by not including a community lament. Instead a recounting of the Exodus has taken its place. The text can be outlined in the following way: (1) divine recounting of the exodus (vv. 16-17), (2) the proclamation of a new salvation (vv. 18-19), and (3) the end result of this new salvation: water in the wilderness, honor to God by creatures, and praise of God by the people of God (vv. 20-21).

The disputation or trial speech separates into (1) an accusation, (2) charges, (3) calling of witnesses, and (4) decision. The unit does not begin with a clear accusation. Instead accusation and charges are implied in the opening lines of the divine speech (vv. 22-24). Israel is called to witness in vv. 26-27 and a decision of destruction is made in v. 28. Verse 25 presents a problem in that it does not really fit the larger context of the trial speech with the emphasis on judgment.

Significance. The lectionary reading presents two somewhat distinct units, and the preacher may wish to focus on one or the other independently. In either case the boundaries of the lectionary text should be adjusted to include entire form-critical units. The central point of the salvation oracle in 43:16-21 is the emphasis on discontinuity between the former things and a new thing that God is about to do. If this becomes the focus for preaching, care must be given to interpret this text in the larger context of Second Isaiah. If read in isolation the salvation oracle looks as though it is a denial of past tradition, since the prophet proclaims, "Do not remember the former things." And, instead, he turns the attention of his audience to a "new thing" that is about "to spring forth." Second Isaiah is a prophet steeped in tradition, who frequently calls Israel to affirm in the present time the power of God that was evident in past events. The contrast between the former things and new thing in 43:16-21 should be interpreted in this vein. Exilic Israel had come to believe that the best was behind them, with the result that past tradition came to embody a lost golden age. The oracle of salvation does not deny the significance of the past Exodus. In fact it is almost as if the description of the Exodus in vv. 16-17 has become part of the divine name (an epithet). Note the syntax of these verses: "Thus says the Lord, who . . . who. . . . " The two subordinate clauses that begin with "who" provide content to the name by describing the past action of God. But God is not content with past laurels. Instead the past provides the framework for new action in the present. The prophet is concerned that exilic Israel not be burdened by the framework of the past, but use it to see a new picture of God's salvation in the present. There certainly is discontinuity in this proclamation. Unforeseen things are about to happen, but these events will be an extension of past tradition and not a departure from it. Salvation will not negate the past Exodus, but add a new chapter to it.

The trial speech in 43:22-28 addresses the problem of the relationship between the past and present from a somewhat different perspective—from the point of view of judgment rather than salvation. The disputation in this text is between God and Israel. Although the entire unit is in first person divine speech, there is an implicit accusation by Israel that is prompting the divine discourse: It is that God's punishment of Israel in bringing them into exile goes far beyond anything they deserved. God's defense of the Exile as punishment is placed in the setting of a trial ("Accuse me, let us go to trial; set forth your case, so that you may be proved right."). The original form-critical unit most likely did not include v. 25 with its introduction of salvation. Instead vv. 22-24, 26-28 are a justification of God's action on the basis of worship. This argument is set forth in vv. 22-24. Israel fails to communicate with God in worship, but uses the occasion to manipulate God. The result was a complete reversal of worship: God was forced to serve the worshipers rather than worship being service to God (The Hebrew of v. 24*b* translates literally, "You made me serve with your sins" which is lost somewhat in the NRSV translation, "You have burdened me with your sins"). Because of this reversal God "profaned the princes of the sanctuary" and "delivered Jacob to utter destruction" (v. 28).

Although this text presents a justification of the Exile, it also introduces a problem of how to move beyond judgment, or, to state the problem differently, of how to move from the past into a new future with God. The introduction of v. 25 into the center of the trial speech addresses the problem of the relationship between the past and the present from the point of view of judgment. The solution picks up the motifs from the salvation oracle. God can save again because past tradition need not be the final word for God. "I will not remember your sins" (v. 25*b*).

The Response: *Psalm 41*

A Song of Thanksgiving

Setting. The genre of Psalm 41 is disputed. Some argue that it is a song of thanksgiving, others a lament of the individual. The choice will determine the setting of the psalm. Is the entire psalm sung by the worshiper who is addressing other worshipers, or is it a liturgy in which a priest addresses an individual who has come to the Temple for healing? The diverse types of language add still further ambiguity in assessing genre. The psalm includes wisdom (vv. 1-3), lament (vv. 5-9), prayer (vv. 4, 10), confidence (vv. 11-12) as well as doxology (v. 13).

Structure. Psalm 41 separates into four parts. It begins in vv. 1-3 with generalized advice to those present before the psalmist shifts to the past time in vv. 4-10 in order to review her illness. Verses 11-12 shift the focus back to the present with statements of confidence, which moves into doxology. The outline illustrates how the psalm moves from present (vv. 1-3) to past (vv. 4-10) and back into the present (vv. 11-13).

Significance. Psalm 41 picks up the problem of interrelating the past and the present that was evident in Isaiah 43, but in a much more personal setting, with the threat of illness. The lament in vv. 5-9 provides a backdrop for seeing how God is able to reverse situations. The psalmist's enemies and friends alike had all lost hope in any recovery of the psalmist. The psalmist builds out from this hopeless situation, first with the words of prayer by the psalmist in vv. 4 and 10, and then with words of confidence and teaching in vv. 1-3 and 11-13, which are the central points of the psalm. God does not give up on the people of God (vv. 2-3), which is evident in the psalmist's reversal of fortunes (vv. 11-12). This emphasis suggests that Psalm 41 be read as a thanksgiving of an individual.

New Testament Texts

In the reading we find that the Corinthians had questions about Paul, as some of Jesus' contemporaries had questions about him. Paul replies by declaring and demonstrating the trustworthiness of God, and Jesus responds by demonstrating his claims to divine authority are backed by divine power. Both texts move from actions to questions to teaching to demonstration.

The Epistle: *II Corinthians 1:18-22*

When the Behavior of Believers Raises Doubts About God

Setting. The situation Paul faced at the time he wrote this letter to the Corinthians was different from that when he penned I Corinthians. After the period and the problem(s) which elicited the first letter, outsiders arrived in Corinth claiming to have the power of God through their relationship to Jesus Christ. Paul calls these people "super-apostles." They taught the Corinthians that Christian faith was a means of access to divine power. They criticized Paul's earlier ministry among the Corinthians in a variety of ways, suggesting his work was inadequate because, they said, he was spiritually weak. Because of this criticism, the members of the Corinthian congregation began to question different aspects of Paul's earlier activities and proclamation. Paul's letter addresses this situation and combats this new problem in several ways.

Structure. The full unit of thought in which the verses of this reading occur is II Corinthians 1:15-22, wherein Paul explains his past actions, which have been criticized by some of the Corinthians. Verses 18-22 seem more "spiritual" than the discussion of travel plans that precedes them in vv. 15-17, but without the concrete context provided by these initial verses, vv. 18-22 may make little sense, or worse, bad sense. Either reading or referring to vv. 15-17 will do no harm to the use of this epistle reading in worship.

In vv. 15-17 Paul raises the issue of whether he has vacillated in changing previously announced travel plans. Verse 18 denies that he was double-minded or undependable because he did make a change. Then, vv. 19-22 become christological, theological, and pneumatological in tone and concern, since doubts about the apostle may have raised doubts about what he had preached and taught among the Corinthians. The designated verses of the lectionary reading correctly suggest moving toward the theological concern of the text, not merely dealing with past problems in the life of the Church; but it is important to notice that Paul's theology is connected here with the very real life of the Corinthian congregation, so that preaching on this text today should aim at relating the articulation of theology to the realities of everyday Christian living.

Significance. The problem Paul faced with the Corinthians when he penned these lines seems fairly mundane; some of them were upset because he had not followed through as he had said he would on his travels plans. The topic is quite practical, and we should not be too unsympathetic to the Corinthians who asked (quite reasonably) why Paul changed his mind. Yet we must be quick to notice how Paul's remarks are steeped in theological language, so that the problem was likely larger than it may initially appear to be.

In I Corinthians 16:5-9 Paul said he would come to Corinth from Macedonia; but, then, he came to Corinth before going to Macedonia and, then, he promised, when he later departed, to return to Corinth. But he didn't! (Other understandings of the specifics of Paul's goings and comings are possible because of the ambiguity of some of the apostle's statements, but that the basic problem between Paul and the Corinthians arose because he did not do exactly what he promised is clear in any case.) Thus at issue is this: Does Paul's apparent ambivalence mean that the gospel he preached is less than reliable? Paul's answer: Indeed not! But one may ask, Why not?

With doubts raised, Paul reiterates the basics of the theology he had communicated to the Corinthians. Verses 19-20 name the Son of God as Jesus the Christ, God's anointed; and, then, remind the Corinthians that Jesus Christ is the fulfillment of all God's promises. Here, Paul does not explain what he means by "promises," but elsewhere in his correspondences with the Corinthians we find him teaching that "in accordance with the scriptures" Christ "died for our sins," "was buried," and "was raised on the third day." All this means the salvation of humanity, for in Jesus Christ God has been and is at work forgiving sin, inaugurating new life, that "God may be all in all." Paul assures the Corinthians that Jesus Christ is the reality of God's promises. In other words, God's promises are not founded on the Apostle Paul and his colleagues, though they have proclaimed God's faithfulness made known in Jesus Christ.

Paul makes clear that the gospel is rooted in God, whose trustworthiness is above question. In order to "prove" his declaration about God's trustworthiness made real in Jesus Christ, Paul cites the evidence of the Holy Spirit whom God has given the Corinthians as an "installment" payment on the larger promise of salvation. Again, in other words, the truth of the gospel rooted in God is known by the Corinthians because of the real workings of God in their lives, not merely because of Paul's preaching and teaching. This is not a theology of experience, but it is a theology that takes experience seriously as a real component of valid (and validating) faith in God. The Corinthians may have confidence in Paul's message because they know the truth of the gospel through the reality of God's presence and power in their lives. The failure (or, success) of other believers is never the final case against (or, for) the reality of the gospel, God, or our own relationship to God.

The Gospel: *Mark 2:1-12*

Jesus Forgives Sins!

Setting. The lesson for this week comes at the outset of the larger section, 2:1–3:35, where Mark records a series of controversies and other stories. More specifically, in 2:1–3:6 we find a set of at least eight stories about Jesus' conflicts with religious authorities, and in these narratives we see that Mark includes several authoritative pronouncements made by Jesus. Several key themes play in these accounts: The authority of Jesus to forgive sins, the freedom of Jesus in his choice of those among whom he works, the true character of Jesus' piety, the innovative nature of Jesus' ministry, and Jesus' attitude toward the Sabbath.

Structure. The basic story is structured in the three-part pattern of an ancient miracle account: problem; solution; confirmation; and, as is usual in miracle stories of the New Testament, there are striking additional elements and concerns that show that the basic story of the miracle has become the vehicle for a message much larger than simply that Jesus did this or that miraculous deed.

Verses 1-2 establish the situation, recalling the initial popular rush to hear the teaching of Jesus. Verses 3-4 narrate the activity of the paralytic and his four friends so that we see the problem. Verse 5 tells of the action of Jesus which begins the solution, but remarkably we are also told that Jesus "saw their faith" and effected the solution to the problem by saying, "Son, your sins are forgiven." Verses 6-10 actually interrupt the basic story of the healing and translate the account into a debate between certain scribes and Jesus about his authority to forgive sins. Verse 11 resumes the normal structure, recording Jesus' further word to the paralytic—healing through a mere word is unusual in ancient miracle stories. Finally, v. 12 gives a double confirmation: the man rises and the crowd reacts. The logic of the story is (1) people in need turn to Jesus; (2) Jesus forgives sins; (3) this is hard for some to believe; (4) nevertheless, it is shown to be true; (5) in amazement, to God be the glory! The dynamics of the account may stimulate the preacher's thinking about the structure of the sermon.

Significance. The issues at the heart of this elaborated miracle story is Jesus' authority and the radical, new, striking character of his activity. The last thing we find Jesus to be is a sweet fellow mumbling pious platitudes. His deeds struck awe and his words caused controversies. We must always remember that no one crucified Jesus for inspiring lofty thoughts and lovely feelings. In everything the gospels record him saying and doing we find his ministry and message to be a call for God's will to be done, and, in turn, he himself claimed to do it. Jesus embodies the doing of God's will, but his radical departure from the norms of traditional piety caused him to be an extraordinarily controversial figure. Thus he attracted a crowd. Some came to listen; some came to see; some came to experience; some came to criticize; and in it all, many were scandalized.

In this story Mark describes Jesus as having a lordly disposition. He was teaching, apparently because he thought he had something to say that was worth hearing. And, then, four friends brought another paralyzed man to present him to Jesus. Mark tells us that in the action Jesus saw their faith. He did not merely see what they did, but why they did it—surely something more than a human reading of the situation. Jesus saw at a theological level.

As he saw, so he acted. Calling the man "son," assuming the position of his "father," Jesus told him his sins were forgiven. Any first-century Jew might have connected sin and sickness; but no other went about doing what all agreed was only God's prerogative—that is, forgiving sins. But Jesus did, and so those in the story supposedly most expert about matters of the divine, the scribes, questioned Jesus' action. Again, Jesus saw at a more than human level into their "hearts"; and in response he demonstrated his authority to do God's work. ("The Son of Man" in first-century Jewish thought was one who would come to execute divine judgment, God's authorized divine agent.)

The man was healed, and he obeyed Jesus' command to get up and go home. In turn, the people of the crowd were amazed; in their amazement, they reacted in a model fashion—they "glorified God."

EPIPHANY 7: THE CELEBRATION

Perhaps the most effective way to begin a program of liturgical renewal in the congregation is to concentrate on that section of today's epistle lesson that says, "For this reason it is through him that we say the 'Amen,' to the glory of God." The restoration of the "Amen" as the work of the people should be the first goal of any liturgical renewal program. If that cannot be achieved, all the rest is probably cosmetic. Ministers saying "Amen" as a signal that the prayer is over help keep the congregation in the dark about their role in the liturgical drama. Preachers who conclude their own sermons with "Amen" offer convincing evidence that they have either never learned or have forgotten the meaning of the word. What sense is there in saying that you agree with what you have just said? Choirs who sing the "Amen" at every point in which it occurs in the service help rob the person in the pew of a rightful participation in the worship of God.

Today's Gospel lesson, coming as it does after last week's lessons with the baptism imagery, which we discussed at that time, leads to the observation that most of the Church's sacramental life is a commentary on the meaning of baptism. The physical healing of the paralytic is connected here with the forgiveness of sins. The physical healing is a sign of a deeper healing of the soul. Healing in the Church is never an end in itself; it is a sign of what God has done for us in our baptisms and continues to do when we confess our post-baptismal sins and seek forgiveness. Confession of sin, whether private or public, when accompanied by true repentance and contrition, and the consequent declaration of pardon is a renewal of our baptism. That is why in some liturgies the absolution is accompanied by sprinkling the congregation with holy water.

The following hymn by Charles Wesley is a beautiful commentary on the Gospel and its application to our own Christian experience.

> Jesus, thy far-extended fame
> My drooping soul exults to hear;
> Thy name, thy all-restoring name,
> Is music in a sinner's ear.
>
> Sinners of old thou didst receive
> With comfortable words and kind,
> Their sorrows cheer, their wants relieve,
> Heal the diseased, and cure the blind.
>
> And art thou not the Savior still,
> In every place and age the same?
> Hast thou forgot thy gracious skill,
> Or lost the virtue of thy name?
>
> Faith in thy changeless name I have;
> The good, the kind physician, thou
> Art able now our souls to save,
> Art willing to restore them now.
>
> Wouldst thou the body's health restore,
> And not regard the sin-sick soul?
> The soul thou lovest yet the more,
> And surely thou shalt make it whole.
>
> My soul's disease, my every sin,
> To thee, O Jesus, I confess;
> In pardon, Lord, my cure begin,
> And perfect it in holiness.

Germany or Maryton are suggested tunes.

Eighth Sunday After Epiphany

Old Testament Texts

Hosea 2:14-20 is a surprising oracle of salvation in the context of an emotional estrangement between husband and wife. Psalm 103:1-13, 22 is a hymn of praise.

The Lesson: *Hosea 2:14-20*

Sex and Salvation

Setting. The Old Testament lesson must be placed in the larger context of Hosea 1–3. A quick overview of these chapters reveals that chapters 1 and 3 are prose, while chapter 2 is poetry. The prose chapters describe Hosea's marriage to a prostitute named Gomer. In Hosea 1 God tells Hosea to marry Gomer and to have children with her. The three children symbolize divine judgment: Jezreel (a place where Israel will be defeated in battle), Loruhamah (meaning, not pitied), and Loammi (meaning, not my people). The children are an occasion for judgment in the marraige of Hosea and Gomer because the prophet is not sure that they are his own. This uncertainty prompts the prophet to file for divorce in chapter 2. Note how the language changes to poetry in Hosea 2 as the identity of the prophetic speaker seems to merge without notice into divine speech. God and Hosea are interchangeable in this parable of Israel's judgment.

The dispute shifts from judgment to salvation, which provides the setting for Hosea 3, where the prophet/God (perhaps) remarries Gomer/Israel. There is much debate in the commentaries concerning the historical prophet Hosea and whether the events alluded to in Hosea 1–3 are fictional or historical. Such debates raise interesting form-critical problems about the identity of the speakers in Hosea 2. For our purposes the central issue for preaching will be to determine how the relationship of Hosea and Gomer suggests commentary on the relationship of God and Israel.

Structure. Hosea takes on the role of a family prosecutor in chapter 2, though the text may or may not have been imagined in a court among the elders at the gate. Note how he complains to his children about his spouse. The prophet begins with a demand that the children "plead with your mother, plead" (v. 2), which moves to a formal divorce declaration that "she is not my wife and I am not her husband" (v. 2) and an initial punishment, "I will strip her naked and expose her as in the day she was born" (v. 3) with evidence, "for their mother has played the whore. . . . For she said, 'I will go after my lovers.' " (v. 5). The remainder of the chapter consists of Gomer's punishment. There are three punishments, which are indicated with the word *therefore* in vv. 6, 9, 14. The lectionary reading is the third and last instance of the sentencing of Gomer. The consequences appear to increase in severity. First, because of her sleeping around, Gomer will be frustrated in any future love affairs (vv. 6-8). The second consequence proven in her behavior is worse. Hosea will no longer support her, and, furthermore, he will expose her as a whore to her lovers (vv. 9-13). Then, just when we expect the final and devastating punishment against Gomer, the consequences emerge in a stunning reversal and re-engagement. Hosea changes his mind and withdraws his divorce decree against his wife. Instead of leaving her, he will allure her back to earlier days, when Gomer was an innocent virgin, in the hope of renewing their marriage (vv. 14-20). This section of the chapter separates into two parts. The first presents the surprising reversal in poetic form (vv. 14-15). The second provides further commentary on this action in narrative form by introducing the motif of covenant (vv. 16-20).

Significance. There is an analogy between sexual fidelity and covenant that is explored in detail in all of the commentaries and the reader is encouraged to take advantage of these resources. Covenant is a legal concept that was used to provide a metaphor for the meaning of salvation in ancient Israel. Salvation is a contract (covenant), which, if not fulfilled for any reason, was no longer binding. In other words, salvation is conditional upon obedience. Law, therefore, was essential for understanding the conditional nature of salvation, and this is carried through in the divorce setting of Hosea 2. The marriage of Hosea and Gomer is commentary on covenant. Marriage is a legal contract in which there were set conditions by which it could be dissolved. Hosea 1–3 presupposes this legal background. But, as we all know, a marriage agreement is not quite the same as other legal contracts. It is law mixed with sex and high emotion.

Hosea changes Israel's understanding of covenant when he removes the concept of covenant from the international law court (where treaties are signed) to the bedroom. In contemporary terms, salvation, therefore, is no longer like signing a thirty-year mortgage on a house in which the legal conditions are material and impersonal. Being saved is marrying God, with the result that worship is so intimate that sexuality becomes a more appropriate metaphor for the relationship than the law court. Two conclusions arise from this. First, faithlessness to God is not the equivalent of missing a mortgage payment on a house. Rather it is more like whoring around. Second, and this is the point of the Old Testament lesson, when covenant shifts from legal decree to love surprising reversals are also possible. Love transcends law and marriages can continue even after the worst infidelities. Too often in preaching Hosea, the sexual background of the book is noted in passing before the analogy to covenant is made and the topic can proceed on safer ground. The power of this book is in the sexual imagery, and it is what must be explored in preaching the prophet's understanding of salvation as marriage to God.

The Response: *Psalm 103:1-13, 22*

A Hymn of Praise

Setting. Psalm 103 is a hymn of praise that mixes personal experience of salvation (vv. 1-5) with broader confessional conclusions about the nature of God (vv. 6-22).

Structure. The lectionary reading includes the first half of the hymn, where the focus is primarily on the nature of God in the light of the psalmist's experience of rescue. Verses 14-18 provide contrast between God and humans on a larger scale, before ending with language of blessing (vv. 19-22) that is similar to vv. 1-2. Verses 1-13 separate into three parts. Verses 1-5 begin with statement of blessing to God (vv. 1-2), which is followed by a series of statements that describe the actions of God. The structure of this section, therefore, is a repetition of "Bless God, who. . . . " Verses 6-10 shift to past tradition (Moses) and formulaic language (God is merciful and gracious . . .) to place the salvific character of God in a larger context. Finally, vv. 11-13 conclude with a series of similes—which are part of the larger confessional formula—to explore in yet another way the love of God.

Significance. The psalm provides excellent commentary on Hosea. It includes many of the motifs that appear in Hosea 2 (the steadfast love of God, the forgiveness of God, and even covenant if the text is extended to v. 18). The movement of the psalm from personal experience to the larger context of tradition provides an avenue for the congregation to appropriate the language of Hosea for themselves. The movement proceeds in the following manner: Bless God, who forgives, heals, redeems, provides love and mercy, and thus satisfies (vv. 1-5), which then allows the congregation to claim the traditional confessional statements about God in vv. 6-13. The reference to Moses is a clear indication that this psalm is quoting Exodus 34:6-9, where the character of God to forgive was first revealed after the incident of the golden calf, a story which itself may also have sexual overtones like Hosea in describing Israel's rejection of God.

New Testament Texts

The texts for this week are related in only the most general theological terms. Paul's words to the Corinthians are concerned with recognizing the real divine source of all power, poise, and proficiency for Christian life. He argues against the claims of others who see themselves rather than God as the locus of power. In Mark, we continue to read of Jesus' controversial early ministry in Galilee. In what he does, what he promotes among his followers, and what he says, Jesus shows himself to be different from other religious leaders of his time and place.

The Epistle: *II Corinthians 3:1-6*

The Confidence and Competence of the New Covenant

Setting. The section of II Corinthians from 2:14–6:13 (or 7:4) is an impassioned plea with the Corinthians in which Paul explains the character of his ministry as consistent with the character of the gospel. Within II Corinthians 2:14–7:4 we find a section of introduction (2:14–3:6), a discussion proper of the substance and style of Paul's ministry (3:7–5:21), and a section of hortatory materials (6:1–7:4). The verses of our reading come at the end of the introductory section of Paul's argument. Recall that Paul is responding to criticism from both the so-called "super-apostles" and some members of the Corinthian congregation.

Structure. The reading falls into two clear parts, vv. 1-3 and vv. 4-6. Paul raised a rhetorical question in 2:16*b*, and he began to answer his query directly in 2:17. In turn, Paul's question-and-answer style in vv. 1-3 is often understood as a "parenthesis" or a slight excursus on the line of his argument in 2:17; whereas Paul returns in vv. 4-6 directly to answering the question posed in 2:16*b*.

Indeed, vv. 1-3 are highly situational, and it is difficult to know how to bring Paul's thought and emotion into play in the formation of sermons. Perhaps, at most, we can see the apostle's involvement and polished rhetorical style and, in turn, seek to emulate such qualities in our own preaching from this text. Then, vv. 4-6—with the themes of "confidence through Christ in God," "competence from God for service," and "the new Christian covenant of life from the Spirit" (prominent among others)—will more likely inspire the substance of sermons.

Significance. Having taken a dialogical approach—that is, posing a rhetorical question and offering an answer for the sake of instructing others in 2:16*b*-17 (an element of style well-known in antiquity from the diatribe-speeches of Stoic and Cynic philosophers)—Paul continues to probe in similar fashion in an aside (vv. 1-3). Yet, even here Paul is pressing the sociological and theological issues with which he is concerned, not merely spinning his verbal wheels. The mention in v. 1 of a "letter of recommendation" probably indicates that those who have come among the Corinthians and criticized Paul themselves possess such authorizing or endorsing documents. Paul declares that the Corinthians are his letter of recommendation, so that he is known to be what he really is, not by what someone says about him but by what he has done and what is known by the experience of the Corinthians. Finally, v. 3 declares that the Corinthian church existed because of the work of the Spirit, obviously mediated through Paul's ministry, not merely because of ink on a page! This contrast allows Paul to move to a second juxtaposition, stone and hearts. *Stone* is an image-play in relation to the Mosaic tablets in Exodus 31, whereas *heart* likely alludes to the divinely promised new covenant of Jeremiah 31:33. The sets of images in these verses seem strange, almost coming "out of the blue," so that interpreters suspect their cryptic character results from Paul's picking up these motifs from his opponents. In any case, vv. 1-3 are highly bound to the situation Paul faced, and one hopes the Corinthians could follow Paul's references more easily than we can from a great distance today.

When Paul returns in vv. 4-6 to answer the question posed in 2:16*b*, he is easier to track. At issue is the source of power, which the opponents claim to possess and which they criticize Paul for either not having or having too little of. Paul's critique of his opponents' claim is clear: He has confidence for life and for doing ministry, not because he is adequate and not because he possesses power, but because God is adequate and because God is the source of power. God is the origin of Paul's work. God enables Paul's ministry, and Paul is never independent from God. The image of thorough dependence upon God communicates the reality of our being related to God so that we may live both confidently and competently. Such genuine, complete relatedness is the substance of the "new covenant." Christians do not merely know God through words, rather believers are in communion with God spiritually through the work of the Spirit. Here, Paul articulates his essential theological conviction, namely that God has primacy in all of Christian life. God has not merely authorized us and sent us off to live independently in confidence and competence; rather, God has grasped our lives through the Spirit and we have a new relationship that establishes and energizes a new way of living in relationship to God and, in turn, in relationship to others.

The Gospel: *Mark 2:13-22*

Striking and Strange Standards and Sayings

Setting. We have seen that Mark 2:1–3:6 is a collection of stories about Jesus' differences with various religious leaders and that several key themes are emphasized through the accounts in this portion of the Gospel. There are but ten verses in our lesson, yet here in rapid succession Mark presents four stories that recall Jesus' freedom in forming community, the motives of his ministry, the distinctiveness of his piety, and the dynamic new quality of his work.

Structure. One may easily discern four units of material in the lesson: the story of the calling of Levi (vv. 13-14), the controversy over eating with tax collectors and sinners (vv. 15-17), the exchange about fasting (vv. 18-20), and the sayings about patches and wineskins (vv. 21-22). Commentators recognize that these traditions have a rich, and still partially discernible, history—perhaps having existed originally as independent accounts in the life of the early Church. Yet we should see that as Mark arranges these stories in his Gospel, they are part of a larger cluster, and within the larger cluster the stories relate to one another in pairs; so that the first and second accounts are related, as are the third and fourth. For preaching, either all four pieces or either pair of accounts will serve well as texts. The specific themes are Jesus' authority and the remarkable, unusual character of his work.

Significance. Those who followed Jesus were not from the usual crowd that took an interest in the teaching of religious authorities, so we should not be surprised that their actions seemed strange to the traditionally devout. What may be a bit surprising, however, is that Jesus himself sought out these people and called them to discipleship. Jesus was the active force in attracting the unusual following. Notice as the lesson opens that Jesus is at work teaching, and the crowd gathered to hear him; but, notice also that Levi, whom Jesus calls to follow, is not in the crowd. Levi was where we might expect him to be—"sitting at the tax booth," showing no evident interest in Jesus' work. But Jesus went to him, a tax collector. It may be unnecessary to explain that tax collectors were not part of polite society, religious or otherwise, in first-century Israel, specifically because as tax collectors they worked for the much resented Romans to collect the more resented taxes. Moreover, tax collectors were considered cheats and thieves, for the word on them was they collected more than was actually due and pocketed the excess. Levi's occupation marginalized him to the fringes (or, beyond) of society. We shouldn't be surprised not to see Levi in the crowd, but we ought to be struck by the unprecedented way in which Jesus calls him, a tax collector, to discipleship.

Through the exchange in the next incident that Mark reports, we learn that Jesus' habit of associating with tax collectors and sinners (this designation may mean no more than that these were everyday folks who simply were not all that concerned with the fine points of religion, not necessarily that they were all that bad) appeared odd to the normal religious leaders. Jesus explained his pattern of relations. He came to those in need, to the sick and to sinners—or, as the old gospel tunes used to put it, to the "sin-sick." In going to Levi, in eating and drinking with tax collectors and sinners, Jesus acted in a way that revealed the depth and the truth of God's love for humanity. God is concerned with all of humankind, and the farther we are from God, the more God is interested in us. In Jesus we see God's love reaching out to call and to embrace us both despite and because of our sinfulness, and we learn that God does not approve of the distance. This is not an "anything goes" approach to life and religion, for as is clear from the complete picture of Jesus' ministry, his call to sinners was a call to righteousness—to a relationship with God and to a life that lives out God's will.

In other ways Jesus' ministry did not fit the norms of his day. For example, his disciples did not fast as did the adherents of other circles of piety. When he explained himself to those who asked him about the failure of his disciples to fast, Jesus spoke with images and metaphors that seem fairly clear to us as readers of Mark's Gospel. His ministry was something new, and it should not be expected to be simply compatible with traditional patterns of piety. Yet, notice his answers claim that his ministry is more than simply novel. There is a declaration of power in his images that forms a commentary on, even a partial condemnation of, the domestication (shrunk cloth) and rigidity (brittle skins) of traditional religion.

Moreover, in his words about the bridegroom (a teaching that is intelligible only from the perspective of the cross and Resurrection) there is both the recognition of the appropriateness of celebration in the presence of Jesus and an anticipation of future times when things will be different. We should see that while we live in celebration of the presence of the bridegroom, as the celebration of the presence of the risen Lord, still we also live in the time of future fasting toward which Jesus' sayings pointed.

EPIPHANY 8: THE CELEBRATION

The Gospel lesson today is divided into three sections (vv. 13-17, 18-20, 21-22); preachers and worship planners may wish to use only one of them in order to keep a clearer focus.

The first section deals with the call of Levi (Matthew) and the discussion about Jesus' mission to sinners. The following collect, adapted from that for St. Matthew's Day in *The Lutheran Book of Worship,* may serve as an opening prayer to prepare for the Gospel lesson:

Almighty God, your Son our Savior called a despised collector of taxes to become one of his disciples. Help us, like Levi, to respond to the transforming call of your Son, and to follow him without delay; who lives and reigns with you and the Holy Spirit, one God, now and forever.

The following stanza by Charles Wesley may serve as a response to this portion of the Gospel lesson:

173

> Outcasts of men [The world's outcasts], to you I call:
> Harlots and publicans and thieves;
> He spreads his arms to embrace you all;
> Sinners alone his grace receive.
> No need of him the righteous have;
> He came the lost to seek and save.

Verses 18-20 remind us that Lent is only ten days away, and so it is time to think again about the function of fasting in the Christian life. Jesus speaks of the time of the absence of the bridegroom (the covenantal image used in the lesson from Hosea) and the fasting which is consequent upon that. Such fasting is a corporate event, it is an event of the Church (the wedding guests), and it has a festive character about it, because the guests know that, in spite of his absence, the bridegroom can be depended upon to show himself. The ambiguity of Christian existence has to be admitted up front: Christ has died, Christ is risen, Christ will come again. We find ourselves between the "is" and the "will," and no declaration of realized eschatology will suffice to keep us from feeling that we are not completely at home in the present age.

Verses 21-22 remind us of the radical character of life in Christ. They can also help us think about the Lenten fast and the Paschal banquet, with their images of clothes and of wine. We are preparing in Lent to move from the sackcloth of penitence to Easter's baptismal robes of righteousness, from hunger and thirst in the wilderness to the joy and vitality of the new life that Christ brings and in which we share at the Lord's Supper. The celebration of the Supper today can help the lessons take flesh in the experience of the congregation.

The Gospel chorus, "Spirit of the Living God," is a fitting response to the epistle lesson. The following Wesley stanza also will serve as transition between the epistle and Gospel readings:

> Come, O thou all-victorious Lord,
> Thy power to us make known;
> Strike with the hammer of thy word,
> And break these hearts of stone.

Azmon complements the text exceedingly well.

Last Sunday After Epiphany (Transfiguration Sunday)

Old Testament Texts

Second Kings 2:1-12 recalls Elijah who is carried off into heaven. Psalm 50:1-6 is a description of theophany.

The Lesson: *II Kings 2:1-12*

Ascension and the Passing On of the Mantle

Setting. Second Kings 2 links the prophetic careers of Elijah and Elisha. The stories of Elijah include I Kings 17–19, 21, and II Kings 1–2. Elisha is first mentioned in I Kings 19:19-21 as a disciple of Elijah, and he returns in the same role in the lectionary text for this Sunday. Stories about Elisha become central from the end of II Kings 2 through the beginning of II Kings 9, and his death is reported in II Kings 13:14-21. The sketch of the distribution of stories about Elijah and Elisha illustrates how there are really two distinct cycles of tradition about each prophet, and that they have now been woven into a larger story by means of the motif of succession.

Structure. Some form of interrelationship has been established between II Kings 1 and 2. Second Kings 1 is a story about Elijah denouncing King Ahaziah, who has injured himself and is seeking divine counsel from the foreign god Baalzebub. Elijah stops the messengers on the way to Baalzebub and predicts the king's death because he did not inquire of the Lord (vv. 1-4). King Ahaziah is upset by the news of his impending death and commands his soldiers to bring Elijah to him (vv. 5-8). The remainder of the chapter describes three groups of fifty soldiers, who approach Elijah sitting on a mountain. As the first two groups approach Elijah, he summarily calls down divine fire upon them (vv. 9-10, 11-12). The captain of the third group breaks this pattern by requesting that the prophet spare his life, at which time an angel of the Lord tells Elijah to go to King Ahaziah and confirm the announcement of his death (vv. 13-16). The chapter ends with King Ahaziah dying (vv. 17-18).

Second Kings 2 is a story about Elijah's ascension into heaven (v. 1). As in II Kings 2, the chapter separates into a three-part sequence, with the third section departing from the stereotyped pattern of the first two. Twice Elijah commands Elisha to depart from him, once at Bethel and a second time at Jericho. In each case Elisha refuses, prophets tell Elisha that Elijah is about to ascend, and Elisha responds by confirming their insight and by telling them to be silent (vv. 2-3, 4-5). The third instance takes place by the Jordan River (vv. 6-8). The stereotyped pattern begins (Elijah commands Elisha to depart, the latter refuses), but then it ceases when Elijah parts the Jordan River with his mantle in the witness of fifty prophets, so that he and Elisha can cross on dry ground. Clearly there is a relationship between the three-part structure of II Kings 1 and II Kings 2, especially between the fifty prophets that witness the crossing and the fifty soldiers that are spared the fire from heaven. The two stories diverge, however, at this point: instead of a king dying in I Kings 1:17-18, I Kings 2:9-12 describes Elijah's ascent into heaven.

Significance. Three themes in II Kings 2:1-12 can be explored for preaching: the relationship of Elijah and Elisha, the exodus imagery in the parting of the Jordan, and the ascension of Elijah.

First, the relationship of Elijah and Elisha. The overview of the Elijah and Elisha texts above illustrates how II Kings 2 is meant to link the two prophets, so that Elisha becomes the successor of Elijah. The boundaries of the lectionary text do not bring this theme to its conclusion, since vv. 13-14 describe how Elisha picked up the mantle of Elijah and then parted the Jordan River. The issue of succession, however, is woven throughout the account of the journey from Bethel through Jericho to the Jordan, and the unwillingness of Elisha to leave Elijah can be probed to explore how prophetic power is transferred.

Second, the exodus imagery. The power of Elijah to divide the waters and to cross the Jordan on dry ground points the reader back to God's salvation of Israel at the Reed Sea. At least two points are being made with the incorporation of this event that can be developed in preaching. First, the imminent power of God to save (and to judge in II Kings 1) is underscored through the work of the prophet. In the traditions of the Exodus, the power of God to control the waters is a sign of divine presence in this world. The repetition of this event signals, at the very least, that the salvation of God is not once and for all, but ongoing in the life of God's prophets. Second, a relationship between Moses-Joshua and Elijah-Elisha is made by having these four characters divide water. The exodus imagery, therefore, not only says something about the presence of God in this world, but it also ties back to the first point about succession. All of these characters embody the power of God to save, and this power is transferable.

Third, the ascension of Elijah. Perhaps the most striking aspect of the story is the ascension of Elijah in the chariot of fire (although the parting of the Jordan River is no small feat, even if it has been done before). The meaning of this imagery is difficult to determine precisely, but it most likely incorporates aspects of Israel's holy war traditions, which were used to describe the character of God's salvation, especially in the Exodus.

II Kings 2:1-12 is a tricky text to use for preaching on Transfiguration Sunday. If the focus is on Elijah, it is a story about an ascension and not about transfiguration. The transfiguration of Jesus is a story about divine imminence. It describes how God, in Christ, is present in this world. Thus the movement of the story of Transfiguration is downward, from heaven to earth, while the movement of II Kings 2:1-12 (when the focus is on Elijah) is just the reverse. It describes how the prophet is taken up out of this world, and how his prophetic spirit is passed on to Elisha. If the focus of interpretation is on this aspect of the story, then the ascension of Jesus with the outpouring of his Spirit on the disciples at the close of Luke's Gospel parallels better the movement of II Kings 2:1-12. The exodus motif does explore the presence of God in our world, and when this motif is viewed from the perspective of Elisha, inner-biblical commentary may be possible—especially between the disciple's perception of Jesus and Elisha's vision of the chariot.

The Response: *Psalm 50:1-6*

A Theophany

Setting. Psalm 50 incorporates much of the imagery of theophany, for it describes an epiphany of God in the setting of worship. The psalm begins by listing three names for God in staccato fashion: Mighty one

(Hebrew, *'el*), God (Hebrew, *'elohim*), and Lord (Hebrew, *yhwh*). The location of this theophany is Zion, and it is for the purpose of God to speak a word of judgment to the people of God, who are gathered for worship. Because the emphasis is on speaking, scholars have characterized Psalm 50 as a prophetic liturgy.

Structure. Psalm 50 opens with a description of theophany in vv. 1-6, which provides the setting for two divine speeches, the first in vv. 7-15 ("Hear, O my people, and I will speak."), and the second in vv. 16-22 ("But to the wicked God says . . . "), and a conclusion in v. 23. The larger structure illustrates how the lectionary text includes only the opening description of theophany.

Significance. The prophetic aspect of Psalm 50 provides insight into transfiguration, for it underscores how the epiphany of God is not an end in itself but leads to a word of judgment. Verse 3 lays the groundwork for linking theophany and judgment, when it states that God does not keep silent. Verses 4-6 call the heavens and earth to witness as God prepares to judge the covenant community. The boundaries of the lectionary text do not include the judgments of God that follow in vv. 7-15 and 16-22. Thus the prophetic word from God has been eliminated. In view of this situation the worship leader may wish to incorporate aspects of the divine speeches in the psalm text.

New Testament Texts

The lessons bring the readings for the season after the Epiphany to a conclusion. Paul struggles with the Corinthians to inform them of the nature of faithful Christian living in relation to the true subject of the gospel, Jesus Christ; whereas Mark recounts the events around the transfiguration of Jesus. Both passages call believers away from personal preoccupations toward the subordination of ourselves to the will of Jesus Christ.

The Epistle: *II Corinthians 4:3-6*

The Character and the Content of the Gospel

Setting. We saw in the epistle reading for the Eighth Sunday After the Epiphany how Paul labors in II Corinthians 2:14–6:13 (or 7:4) to explain to the Corinthians that the character of his ministry is consistent with the character of the gospel. Within this larger portion of the letter, 3:7–4:6 is a discussion of Christian life as "serving in the context of the new covenant." Here, Paul discusses Christian service in a polemical manner that argues from Paul's theology in relation to the specific situation in Corinth.

Structure. The verses of the lesson are part of a coherent statement in 4:1-6. Verses 1-4 tell both what Paul does not do as a Christian apostle and what he does do, and he explains why some are unable to grasp the truth of the gospel as he proclaims it. Then, in vv. 5-6 Paul restates even more bluntly in a negative/positive pairing of statements the nature of his work.

Preaching is usually most beneficial when it has clear, strong positive content; but, as anyone who has watched emotionally charged televangelists knows, a little preaching against something can be quite engaging and go a long way! Thus an effective (and accurate) sermon based on this lesson could reflect both the negative and positive dimensions of the text along the lines of these themes: What is not and is appropriate Christian behavior, and what is not and is the subject of the gospel. The frame for this message is seen in vv. 1 and 6—the content of the gospel and the character of Christian life are both given by the grace of God.

Significance. In the midst of the controversy in Corinth Paul explains his message and ministry. The lesson builds on the previous sections of the letter which spoke of the hope of the enduring new covenant and the boldness instilled in believers by God's transforming power. Having stated in 4:1-2 what he does not do, what he does, and why, Paul continues in v. 3 declaring that the only veil related to his work is the inability of some to perceive the validity of his ministry. The reference to being "veiled" is an image playback to the discussion in chapter 3. While the argument here is difficult and complex, Paul is saying that the claims of those who oppose him are the evidence of their own spiritual perversity. Paul explains the lack of perception or appreciation as resulting from the work of "the god of this age." In other words, Satan blinds the unbeliever. This explanation is part of Paul's worldview of apocalyptic dualism. While one preaching in the twentieth century will find (1) merely repeating Paul's lines less than gratifying and (2) attempting to translate (demythologize!) into a contemporary worldview challenging, what must be recognized is that Paul takes the struggle between God and evil with the utmost seriousness. Thus he understands that God's work in this world for the salvation of humankind is a costly, difficult endeavor.

In the remarks of vv. 5-6 we learn that Paul does not consider himself as the appropriate subject of Christian proclamation; rather, he preaches

Christ as Lord. In the secondary level of the statement Paul locates himself in what he declares to be an appropriate Christian role—namely, in service to other believers for the sake of Jesus. Thus Paul maintains the priority of the Lord in ministry, but he shows that holding Jesus high means that one's interest in others will be greater than in oneself. Naming "Jesus" in this statement recalls the real human career of our Lord who lived a life of selfless sacrificial self-giving. Paul concludes his thoughts in this passage by declaring again that God is the source of his apostolic labors (see 2:14, 17; 3:5-6; 4:1; etc.).

The text is an urgent plea for appropriating the true meaning of the Lordship of Jesus Christ in our lives. If he is our Lord, then we are his disciples, followers, and servants. If he gave himself fully for the sake of others, what can it mean to be under his lordship but that we do the same? In discipleship to Jesus Christ we shun behavior designed primarily for our own benefit. As we put Christ ahead of ourselves, in turn, others rise to a new level of importance comparable to Christ's own valuing of them. In the community of Christian faith, by the mercy of God, we are called to new patterns of relatedness that mean mutual concern and support because we all put one another ahead of ourselves.

The Gospel: *Mark 9:2-9*

"Listen to Him"

Setting. The middle portion of Mark's Gospel, from 8:22 through 10:52, contains some of the most dramatic words and events of Jesus' ministry. The section opens and closes with different stories about Jesus' healings of blind men. Commentators often describe these healings as paradigms of the faith experience of the disciples who move through the Gospel from blindness to half-sight to seeing all things clearly; and, then, after they have thrown off the mantle of their ignorance through a full encounter with the Lord, they are able to follow him in the way which is his. Whether this helpful, but essentially allegorical, interpretation of the boundary-stories of the middle portion of Mark is correct, it is certainly the case that Mark 8:22–10:52 contains important information about the identity of Christ and true discipleship to him.

Structure. The story begins with both an enigmatic temporal reference (why does Mark bother to tell us the Transfiguration occurred "after six days"?) and a report of Jesus' separating himself and three special disciples from the crowds and even the other disciples. These elements focus the narrative and give striking intensity to the story. As the account unfolds we find a series of actions and reactions: Jesus is transfigured; Elijah and Moses appear and converse with Jesus; Peter speaks to Jesus; a cloud appears and a voice comes out of the cloud; and suddenly Jesus and the three disciples are left alone. With all this activity the characters change rapidly, but we should not ignore that Jesus is present or referred to in each stage of the story. The show-stopping word from the cloud makes clear the essential focus of the account on Jesus, and then we are left with the three disciples and Jesus alone. From the structure of the story one may be led in proclamation to deal with themes such as (1) the glory of Christ, (2) the realization of the promises of the prophets and the law in Jesus, (3) well meant but essentially ignorant reactions to God's work in Jesus Christ, (4) God's public affirmation of Jesus, (5) the authority of Jesus Christ, and (6) the relation of disciples to Christ.

Significance. After the dramatic beginning of the story, the setting on the mountain should remind anyone familiar with the Old Testament (or others conversant with ancient stories about "the gods") of dramatic scenes of divine revelation (Sinai, Horeb, and Zion; or Olympus, the Acropolis, and Acrocorinth). The whole story of the Transfiguration is surely a prefigurement of the resurrection fate of Jesus who has only recently begun to speak of his forthcoming crucifixion to the disciples.

As we imagine our way into this text, there is one truly valid point of identification for us. Since we are not Jesus, Elijah, or Moses, and since we certainly are not God Almighty (seen in the symbols of the cloud and the heavenly voice), we find an identity within the account as we stand with Peter, James, and John. What an amazing sight they see—a combination of heaven and earth, a blending of time and eternity, a mixture of reality and transcendence, a merging of history and theology.

How does one preach about this glimpse of holiness? The text overwhelms the preacher with its flood of images, themes, characters, and incidents. The last thing one approaching this text for proclamation should do is to attempt to explain the story—and thus to explain the Transfiguration away! The best rationalistic (and rationalizing) nineteenth-century scholarship could do was to suggest that this narrative must be a misplaced post-Resurrection story, an explanation intended pathetically both to affirm and to deny the veracity of the account. The mood of our so-called "post-modern" age may be a better one for interpreting this story.

As we stand with the disciples, we share with them their ignorance for fully comprehending these events. Yet we are not left purely baffled. The voice of God gives us definite insight and directions: Jesus Christ is God's beloved son, and we are to heed his words. Under the authority of Christ and in obedience to his teaching, we are called to live our lives. We are not left to fumble through life merely doing the best we can, right or wrong! God's love is made flesh and God's will is given voice in Jesus Christ, and as believers we are given the certitude of living by listening to him.

THE TRANSFIGURATION: THE CELEBRATION

Transfiguration Sunday is always the Last Sunday After Epiphany, regardless of how many Sundays that may be. Today's lessons remind us that the post-Epiphany time has been characterized by the theme of the light of God in Christ breaking upon the world. In this final epiphany before the beginning of Lent, Christ is seen by the disciples in dazzling splendor, the Transfiguration a prefiguration of his Resurrection glory. And the epistle lesson speaks of "the light of the knowledge of the glory of God in the face of Jesus Christ." The psalm speaks of God shining forth in a perfection of beauty. "Fairest Lord Jesus" and "Christ, Whose Glory Fills the Skies" are particularly appropriate hymns for today. Because of the inclusion of this Sunday as a special observance in the lectionary, most recent hymnals have included one or more hymns that have special relevance to the Transfiguration.

The Old Testament lesson is chosen allegorically to emphasize Jesus as the successor to and fulfillment of Israel's prophetic tradition as symbolized by Elijah. The issue as to whether or not it is a transfiguration or an ascension narrative (see Old Testament commentary) should not be a particular concern for the preacher, since it is the person of Elijah as prophet in general that we are interested in rather than any single account about him. The lesson has been chosen because it narrates a theophany involving Elijah who also appears in the theophany we call the Transfiguration. He stands with Moses who represents the tradition of the Law (and who is the subject of the Old Testament lesson on this Sunday in Years A and C). Their appearance together witnesses to Jesus as the fulfillment of the law and the prophets. For those who have been doing a series of sermons on the meaning of preaching during these weeks, attention could be directed to the centrality of Jesus for Christian preaching. It is his words to which we are to listen, and his message which we are to proclaim. He is the lens through which we read and interpret the law and the prophets.

Today's Gospel lesson takes us back to the First Sunday After Epiphany, the Baptism of the Lord, because of the voice from the cloud confirming the identity of Jesus. At the baptism it is not made clear if onlookers hear the voice. The additional exhortation, "listen to him," in today's narrative suggests that the theophany had been for Jesus alone at the baptism, and now it is extended to disciples who are forbidden to tell what they have seen until after the Resurrection (v. 9). This moment of glory can only be understood in terms of the greater glory of the Resurrection, but the crucifixion stands as the interpretive hinge. Thus it is that we move in three days from this celebration to the solemn observance of Ash Wednesday.

Scripture Index

Old Testament

New Testament

A Comparison of Major Lectionaries

YEAR B: ADVENT SUNDAY THROUGH THE LAST SUNDAY AFTER THE EPIPHANY

	Old Testament	Psalm	Epistle	Gospel
	THE FIRST SUNDAY OF ADVENT			
RCL	Isa. 64:1-9	80:1-7, 17-19	I Cor. 1:3-9	Mark 13:24-37
RoCath	Isa. 63:16-17, 19; 64:2-7	80:2-3, 15-16, 18-19		Mark 13:33-37
Episcopal	Isa. 64:1-9a	80	I Cor. 1:1-9	
Lutheran	Isa. 63:16b-17; 64:1-8	80:1-7		Mark 13:33-37
	THE SECOND SUNDAY OF ADVENT			
RCL	Isa. 40:1-11	85:1-2, 8-13	II Pet. 3:8-15a	Mark 1:1-8
RoCath	Isa. 40:1-5, 9-11	85:9-14	II Pet. 3:8-14	
Episcopal		85	II Pet. 3:8-15a, 18	
Lutheran		85	II Pet. 3:8-14	

	Old Testament	Psalm	Epistle	Gospel
THE THIRD SUNDAY OF ADVENT				
RCL	Isa. 61:1-4, 8-11	126	I Thess. 5:16-24	John 1:6-8, 19-28
RoCath	Isa. 61:1-2, 10-11	Luke 1:46-50, 53-54		
Episcopal	Isa. 65:17-25	126	I Thess. 5:12-28	
Lutheran	Isa. 61:1-3, 10-11	Luke 1:46*b*-55		
THE FOURTH SUNDAY OF ADVENT				
RCL	II Sam. 7:1-11, 16	Luke 1:47-55	Rom. 16:25-27	Luke 1:26-38
RoCath	II Sam. 7:1-5, 8-11, 16	89:2-5, 27, 29		
Episcopal	II Sam. 7:4, 8-16	132		
Lutheran		89:1-4, 14-18		
CHRISTMAS EVE/DAY (Second Proper)				
RCL	Isa. 62:6-12	97	Titus 3:4-7	Luke 2:(1-7) 8-20
RoCath	Isa. 62:11-12	97:1, 6-7, 11-12		Luke 2:15-20
Episcopal	Isa. 62:6-7, 10-12			
Lutheran	Isa. 52:7-10		Heb. 1:1-9	John 1:1-14

	Old Testament	Psalm	Epistle	Gospel
THE FIRST SUNDAY AFTER CHRISTMAS				
RCL	Isa. 61:10–62:3	148	Gal. 4:4-7	Luke 2:22-40
RoCath	Sirach 3:2-6, 12-14	128:1-5	Col. 3:12-21	
Episcopal		147	Gal. 3:23-25; 4:4-7	John 1:1-18
Lutheran	Isa. 45:22-25		Col. 3:12-17	Luke 2:25-40
JANUARY 1/ HOLY NAME OF JESUS				
RCL	Num. 6:22-27	8	Gal. 4:4-7 or Phil. 2:5-13	Luke 2:15-21
RoCath	Jan. 1 is observed as the Solemnity of Mary by Roman Catholics.			
Episcopal	Exod. 34:1-8		Rom. 1:1-7	
Lutheran			Rom. 1:1-7 or Phil. 2:9-13	Luke 2:21
THE SECOND SUNDAY AFTER CHRISTMAS				
RCL	Jer. 31:7-14	147:12-20	Eph. 1:3-14	John 1:1-18
RoCath	Sirach 24:1-4, 8-12	147:12-15, 19-20	Eph. 1:3-6, 15-18	Matt. 2:13-15, 19-23 or Luke 2:41-52 or Matt. 2:1-12
Episcopal		84	Eph. 1:3-6, 15-19*a*	
Lutheran	Isa. 61:10-62:3		Eph. 1:3-6, 15-18	

	Old Testament	Psalm	Epistle	Gospel
	THE EPIPHANY OF THE LORD			
	(January 6 or the Sunday before)			
RCL	Isa. 60:1-6	72:1-7, 10-14	Eph. 3:1-12	Matt. 2:1-12
RoCath		72:1-2, 7-8, 10-13	Eph. 3:2-3, 5-6	
Episcopal	Isa. 60:1-6, 9	72		
Lutheran		72	Eph. 3:2-12	
	THE BAPTISM OF THE LORD			
	(First Sunday After the Epiphany)			
RCL	Gen. 1:1-5	29	Acts 19:1-7	Mark 1:4-11
RoCath	Isa. 42:1-4, 6-7	29:1-4, 9-10	Acts 10:34-38	Mark 1:7-11
Episcopal	Isa. 42:1-9	89:1-29	Acts 10:34-38	Mark 1:7-11
Lutheran	Isa. 42:1-7	45:7-9	Acts 10:34-38	
	SECOND SUNDAY AFTER THE EPIPHANY			
RCL	I Sam. 3:1-10 (11-20)	139:1-6, 13-18	I Cor. 6:12-20	John 1:43-51
RoCath	I Sam. 3:3-10, 19	40:2, 4, 7-10	I Cor. 6:13-15, 17-20	John 1:35-42
Episcopal		63:1-8	I Cor. 6:11b-20	
Lutheran	I Sam. 3:1-10	67		

	Old Testament	Psalm	Epistle	Gospel
	THIRD SUNDAY AFTER THE EPIPHANY			
RCL	Jonah 3:1-5, 10	62:5-12	I Cor. 7:29-31	Mark 1:14-20
RoCath		25:4-9		
Episcopal	Jer. 3:21–4:2	130	I Cor. 7:17-23	
Lutheran		62:6-14		
	FOURTH SUNDAY AFTER THE EPIPHANY			
RCL	Deut. 18:15-20	111	I Cor. 8:1-13	Mark 1:21-28
RoCath		95:1-2, 6-9	I Cor. 7:32-35	
Episcopal			I Cor. 8:1b-13	
Lutheran		1		
	FIFTH SUNDAY AFTER THE EPIPHANY			
RCL	Isa. 40:21-31	147:1-11, 20c	I Cor. 9:16-23	Mark 1:29-39
RoCath	Job 7:1-4, 6-7	147:1-6	I Cor. 9:16-19, 22-23	
Episcopal	II Kings 4:(8-17) 18-21 (22-31) 32-37	142		
Lutheran	Job 7:1-7	147:1-13		

	Old Testament	Psalm	Epistle	Gospel
SIXTH SUNDAY AFTER THE EPIPHANY				
RCL	II Kings 5:1-14	30	I Cor. 9:24-27	Mark 1:40-45
RoCath	Lev. 13:1-2, 44-46	32:1-2, 5, 11	I Cor. 10:31–11:1	
Episcopal	II Kings 5:1-15a	42		
Lutheran		32		
SEVENTH SUNDAY AFTER THE EPIPHANY				
RCL	Isa. 43:18-25	41	II Cor. 1:18-22	Mark 2:1-12
RoCath	Isa. 43:18-19, 21-22, 24-25	41:2-5, 13-14		
Episcopal		32		
Lutheran				
EIGHTH SUNDAY AFTER THE EPIPHANY				
RCL	Hosea 2:14-20	103:1-13, 22	II Cor. 3:1-6	Mark 2:13-22
RoCath	Hosea 2:16-17, 21-22	103:1-4, 8, 10, 12-13		Mark 2:18-22
Episcopal	Hosea 2:14-23	103	II Cor. 3:(4-11) 17–4:2	Mark 2:18-22
Lutheran	Hosea 2:14-16 (17-18) 19-20	103:1-13	II Cor. 3:1b-6	Mark 2:18-22

THE LAST SUNDAY AFTER THE EPIPHANY
(Transfiguration Sunday)

	Old Testament	Psalm	Epistle	Gospel
RCL	II Kings 2:1-12	50:1-6	II Cor. 4:3-6	Mark 9:2-9
RoCath	The Roman Catholic Church observes the Transfiguration on the Second Sunday in Lent. Today it continues to use the sequence of proper lessons for ordinary time.			
Episcopal	I Kings 19:9-18	27	II Pet. 1:16-19 (20-21)	
Lutheran	II Kings 2:1-12a		II Cor. 3:12–4:2	

A Liturgical Calendar

Advent Through Epiphany   1992–2001

	1992-93 A	1993-94 B	1994-95 C	1995-96 A	1996-97 B
Advent 1	Nov. 29	Nov. 28	Nov. 27	Dec. 3	Dec. 1
Advent 2	Dec. 6	Dec. 5	Dec. 4	Dec. 10	Dec. 8
Advent 3	Dec. 13	Dec. 12	Dec. 11	Dec. 17	Dec. 15
Advent 4	Dec. 20	Dec. 19	Dec. 18	Dec. 24	Dec. 22
Christmas 1	Dec. 27	Dec. 26	Jan. 1	Dec. 31	Dec. 29
Christmas 2	Jan. 3	Jan. 2	- - - - - -	- - - - - -	Jan. 5
Epiphany 1	Jan. 10	Jan. 9	Jan. 8	Jan. 7	Jan. 12
Epiphany 2	Jan. 17	Jan. 16	Jan. 15	Jan. 14	Jan. 19
Epiphany 3	Jan. 24	Jan. 23	Jan. 22	Jan. 21	Jan. 26
Epiphany 4	Jan. 31	Jan. 30	Jan. 29	Jan. 28	Feb. 2
Epiphany 5	Feb. 7	Feb. 6	Feb. 5	Feb. 4	- - - - - -
Epiphany 6	Feb. 14	- - - - - -	Feb. 12	Feb. 11	- - - - - -
Epiphany 7	- - - - - -	- - - - - -	Feb. 19	- - - - - -	- - - - - -
Epiphany 8	- - - - -	- - - - -	- - - - -	- - - - -	- - - - -
Last Sunday	Feb. 21	Feb. 13	Feb. 26	Feb. 18	Feb. 9

	1997-98 C	1998-99 A	1999-2000 B	2000-01 C
Advent 1	Nov. 30	Nov. 29	Nov. 28	Dec. 3
Advent 2	Dec. 7	Dec. 6	Dec. 5	Dec. 10
Advent 3	Dec. 14	Dec. 13	Dec. 12	Dec. 17
Advent 4	Dec. 21	Dec. 20	Dec. 19	Dec. 24
Christmas 1	Dec. 28	Dec. 27	Dec. 26	Dec. 31
Christmas 2	Jan. 4	Jan. 3	Jan. 2	- - - - - -
Epiphany 1	Jan. 11	Jan. 10	Jan. 9	Jan. 7
Epiphany 2	Jan. 18	Jan. 17	Jan. 16	Jan. 14
Epiphany 3	Jan. 25	Jan. 24	Jan. 23	Jan. 21
Epiphany 4	Feb. 1	Jan. 31	Jan. 30	Jan. 28
Epiphany 5	Feb. 8	Feb. 7	Feb. 6	Feb. 4
Epiphany 6	Feb. 15	- - - - - -	Feb. 13	Feb. 11
Epiphany 7	- - - - - -	- - - - - -	Feb. 20	Feb. 18
Epiphany 8	- - - - - -	- - - - - -	Feb. 27	- - - - - -
Last Sunday	Feb. 22	Feb. 14	Mar. 5	Feb. 25